# THE NATURAL LAW

# The Natural Law

*According to Aquinas and Suárez*

Walter Farrell, O.P.

*Edited and with an Introduction by*
Cajetan Cuddy, O.P.

*A thesis, being an examination into the two chief Christian theories of law and a determination of the value of each, presented to the Faculty of Theology of the University of Fribourg, Switzerland, to obtain the degree of Doctor.*

CLUNY
*Providence, Rhode Island*

*"Among all human pursuits, the pursuit of wisdom*
*is more perfect, more noble, more useful,*
*and more full of joy."*

-Saint Thomas Aquinas,
*Summa contra Gentiles*

* * *

# Thomist Tradition

## Book Series

While his birth and death and everything in between remain confined to the thirteenth century, the intellectual legacy of St. Thomas Aquinas perdures to the present day. The Catholic Church continues to recognize the sapiential fecundity of this Doctor whom she invokes as "Common" and "Universal." God gave to the world through the wisdom of his Thomas a gift that does not expire.

There was only one Thomas. However, there have been many Thomists—philosophers and theologians who have assimilated the principles of his instruction and found the freedom that only the truth can provide.

The Thomist Tradition book series from Cluny Media arises from a dual conviction: (1) the thought of St. Thomas Aquinas contains an incomparable fullness of wisdom, and (2) the writings of the Thomists who followed him play a necessary role in mediating his wisdom to subsequent generations. Admittedly, those figures who constitute the Thomist tradition were by no means equals in regard to talent, influence, and renown. Moreover, their individual and collective contributions to the Thomist tradition elude facile comprehension or easy summary. Nonetheless, this series attempts to make available the key texts of figures—both classic and contemporary, major and minor—who rightly claim membership in the living tradition which bears the intellectual imprint of their master, Thomas.

The THOMIST TRADITION series makes these books available not merely as static works of antiquated value or anachronistic interest. Rather, the series is the fruit of our conviction that each Thomist has participated in a legacy perennially alive and perpetually relevant. Under this inspiration, each carefully selected volume in the series includes a new introduction that explains the book's original historical and speculative context. These introductions also outline their volume's enduring relevance to contemporary questions and disputes. Finally, the texts themselves have undergone extensive editorial review and certain footnotes have been added in order to highlight, explain, and clarify themes and passages of particular significance.

It is our sincere hope that this endeavor from Cluny Media will contribute to the renewed interest in the Thomist tradition among contemporary philosophers and theologians. For 800 years, Thomas and the Thomists have demonstrated unparalleled service in the defense and exposition of the saving truth Christ confided to his bride, the Catholic Church. The THOMIST TRADITION book series is designed both to honor that service and to provide the Thomists of today and tomorrow with resources for their own service to the Truth who sets us free.

*Cajetan Cuddy, O.P.*
*General Editor*

THOMIST T☀T TRADITION

Cluny Media edition, 2019

Publisher's Note for the New Edition:
The changes given in the errata page that appears
in the original 1930 edition have been incorporated into this edition.

Originally published by St. Dominic's Press, Ditchling, 1930,
as *The Natural Moral Law According to St. Thomas and Suarez*

For more information regarding this title
or any other Cluny Media publication,
please write to info@clunymedia.com, or to
Cluny Media, P.O. Box 1664, Providence, RI 02901

VISIT US ONLINE AT WWW.CLUNYMEDIA.COM



Nihil obstat: Fr. Dominicus M. Prümmer, O.P., S.T.M.,
and Fr. Andreas Gigon, O.P., S.T.L.

Imprimatur: Fr. Raymundus Meagher, O.P., S.T.L.,
*Prior Provincialis*

Neo-Eboraci, die 30 Juni, 1930

ISBN: 978-1949899467

Cover design by Clarke & Clarke
Cover image: Giovanni di Paolo, *The Expulsion from Paradise*
(detail), 1445, tempera and gold on wood
Courtesy of The Metropolitan Museum of Art, New York

# Contents

* * *

# Introduction for the 2019 Edition

## Foundational Themes in Aquinas's Natural Law Doctrine

*The Natural Law According to Aquinas and Suárez* is the third volume in the THOMIST TRADITION book series. Previously published members of the series considered the relationship between the existence of God and the philosophical science of metaphysics, as well as the nature of theological science in the context of Catholic thought and life.[1] The present text, originally a doctoral dissertation submitted to a Thomistic theological faculty,[2] examines the natural law doctrine of St. Thomas Aquinas (1225–1274) and Francisco Suárez, S.J., (1548–1617). The conclusions proffered in the following pages attempt to achieve fidelity to the former and dissonance with the latter. Farrell would go on to enjoy a certain standing in the intellectual culture characteristic of American Catholicism in the early to mid-twentieth century.[3]

This is a short book. It is not, however, an easy one. *The Natural Law According to Aquinas and Suárez* does not enjoy the same degree of readability as Fr. Farrell's later writings (and those for which he is most known). Nonetheless, it remains a valuable study of an important topic. Indeed, its original inspiration remains applicable to our own time: "The subject of the Natural Moral Law is attracting a great deal of attention today in the fields of Catholic philosophy and theology as well as in the natural sciences, such as anthropology."[4] Farrell goes on to observe

---

1. Thomas C. O'Brien, O.P., *Metaphysics and the Existence of God*, ed. Cajetan Cuddy, O.P. (Providence, RI: Cluny Media, 2017); Joseph Clifford Fenton, *What Is Sacred Theology?*, ed. Cajetan Cuddy, O.P. (Providence, RI: Cluny Media, 2018).
2. Walter Farrell, O.P., *The Natural Moral Law According to St. Thomas and Suárez* (Ditchling: St. Dominic's Press, 1930). This dissertation was submitted to the University of Fribourg, Switzerland.
3. Walter Raphael Farrell (1902–1951) is perhaps best known as the author of the bestselling, four-volume *A Companion to the Summa* (New York: Sheed & Ward, 1939–1941). He was also the founder of the speculative quarterly *The Thomist* (in 1939). Known for the acuity of his thought and the accessibility of his prose, Fr. Farrell was a "pioneer in the teaching of theology to the laity" ("Obituary: The Very Reverend Raphael Walter Farrell, O.P., S.T.M.," *Dominicana*, Vol. 37, No. 1 [1952]: pp. 56–58 [p. 57]). His concise, "pocketbook" presentation of Catholic doctrine remains in print to the present day (*My Way of Life: Pocket Edition of St. Thomas—The Summa Simplified for Everyone* [Brooklyn: Confraternity of the Precious Blood, 1952]).
4. Walter Farrell, O.P., *The Natural Law According to Aquinas and Suárez*, ed. Cajetan Cuddy O.P. (Providence, RI: Cluny Media, 2019), p. xli. For various accounts of the history and status of natural law theory see Thomas E. Davitt, S.J., *The Nature of Law* (St. Louis, MO: B. Herder Book, Co., 1951); Robert P. George, ed., *Natural Law Theory: Contemporary Essays* (Oxford: Oxford University Press, 1994); Pamela M. Hall, *Narrative and the Natural Law: An Interpretation of Thomistic Ethics* (Notre Dame, IN: University of Notre Dame Press, 1994); Anthony J. Lisska, *Aquinas's Theory of Natural Law: An Analytic Reconstruction* (Oxford: Clarendon Press, 1996); Heinrich A. Rommen, *The Natural Law: A Study in Legal and Social History and Philosophy* (Indianapolis, IN: Liberty Fund, 1998); Pauline C. Westerman, *The Disintegration of Natural Law Theory* (Leiden: Brill, 1998); Jean Porter, *Natural and Divine Law: Reclaiming the Tradition for Christian Ethics* (Grand Rapids, MI: William B. Eerdmans Publishing Co., 1999); Christopher Kaczor, *Proportionalism and the Natural Law Tradition* (Washington, DC: The Catholic University of America Press, 2002); Russell Hittinger, *The First Grace: Rediscovering the Natural Law*

"a phenomenon of peoples abandoning Christianity, and sometimes even turning to rank atheism, yet maintaining a definite moral code, frequently in open violation of all laws of logic. This has prompted the question as to whether this morality was the result of an unconscious Christian heritage or whether it flowed from nature itself, from a source that no amount of rhetoric could influence."[5] Although this was certainly true in 1930, we might suggest that it is even more true in 2019.[6]

The following analysis attempts to engage the various elements which belong to any adequate consideration of Thomistic natural law theory. As noted above, this book—like its topic—eludes facile comprehension. And in order to facilitate our appropriation of Farrell's argument, this introductory chapter attempts to outline some of the significant speculative themes found (and sometimes presupposed) in *The Natural Law According to Aquinas and Suárez.*

* * *

*in a Post-Christian World* (Wilmington, DE: ISI Books, 2003); Ana Marta González, *Contemporary Perspectives on Natural Law: Natural Law as a Limiting Concept* (Burlington, VT: Ashgate Publishing Co., 2008); Luis Cortest, *The Disfigured Face: Traditional Natural Law and Its Encounter with Modernity* (New York: Fordham University Press, 2008); Lawrence S. Cunningham, ed., *Intractable Disputes about the Natural Law: Alasdair MacIntyre and Critics* (Notre Dame, IN: University of Notre Dame Press, 2009); James F. Keenan, S.J., *A History of Catholic Moral Theology in the Twentieth Century: From Confessing Sins to Liberating Consciences* (London: Continuum, 2010); and Charles Curran, *The Development of Moral Theology: Five Strands* (Washington, DC: Georgetown University Press, 2013).

5. Farrell, *The Natural Law According to Aquinas and Suárez*, p. xlii.

6. For a direct and engaging response to some of these movements in their contemporary expression, see Edward Feser, *The Last Superstition: A Refutation of the New Atheism* (South Bend, IN: St. Augustine's Press, 2008).

## I. Teleology and the Natural Law

The twentieth-century Thomist Yves Simon once observed that "the theory of natural law, attacked and rejected many times, always comes back with fresh energy."[7] His defense of this claim was that "there would be no eternal return of natural law without an everlasting opposition to natural law."[8] In addition to opposition, the natural law has been subject to much controversy. Questions, doubts, and confusion about the nature of the natural law are quite common within the history of Catholic theology in general and studies of Aquinas's account of the natural law in particular. However, most of the objections arise from two fundamental questions: (1) How is the natural law *known* naturally? and (2) Just how *natural* is the natural law? Does the natural law enjoy an inherent connection to the order of grace and if so how does the integration between them play out? The classicist philosopher Leo Strauss expresses this difficulty clearly: "The ultimate consequence of the Thomistic view of natural law is that natural law is practically inseparable not only from natural theology—i.e., from a natural theology which is, in fact, based on belief in biblical revelation—but even from revealed theology."[9] If the natural law is "practically inseparable" from

7. Yves R. Simon, *The Tradition of Natural Law: A Philosopher's Reflections* (New York: Fordham University Press, 1992), p. 3.

8. Ibid., p. 4. For an insightful summary of Yves Simon's book, see Steven A. Long, "Yves Simon's Approach to Natural Law," *The Thomist*, Vol. 59, No. 1 (1995): pp. 125–35.

9. Leo Strauss, *Natural Right and History* (Chicago: University of Chicago Press, 1950), p. 164. For more on the theological nature of the natural law, see Cajetan Cuddy, O.P., "Thomas Aquinas on the Bible and Morality: The Sacred Scriptures, the Natural Law, and the Hermeneutic of Continuity," in *Towards a Biblical Thomism: Thomas Aquinas and the Renewal of Biblical Theology*, ed. Jörgen Vijgen and Piotr Roszak (Pamplona: EUNSA, 2018), pp. 173–97.

revealed theology, then, again, one is led to ask: in what sense is it *natural*?[10]

In order to begin to answer these questions, we must analyze the essential teaching about the natural law found within the writings of Aquinas and in Pope St. John Paul II's 1993 encyclical *Veritatis Splendor*. Such an analysis reveals that the "inclination" evident in the natural constitution of all contingent beings is a teleological order divinely *impressed* on all created reality. All being is *per se* inclinational, intentional, and ordered to its properly proportioned end. Thus, all being is constituted with (and in) a *natural teleology*. The natural-teleological order of all being becomes *natural law teleology* when the natural teleology is assumed and practically applied by *reason*. Only the rational creature is able to participate in the eternal *ratio* of God under the formal aspect of *ratio*—in other words, only the rational creature can claim a properly *ratio-nal* participation. Additionally, this type of creature is uniquely able to grasp formally the eternal law of God as *God's law*. Hence *Veritatis Splendor* uses the word "theonomic" to describe the natural law: Through reason, the human person is able to recognize the formal integrity of the eternal law of God as both *theological* and *legal*, and thus appears the full theonomic nature of the natural law. Teleology is the essential foundation of the natural law.

10. See Romanus Cessario, O.P., "Why Aquinas Locates the Natural Law within the *Sacra Doctrina*," in *St. Thomas Aquinas and the Natural Law Tradition: Contemporary Perspectives*, eds. John Goyette, Mark S. Latkovic, and Richard S. Myers (Washington, DC: The Catholic University of America Press, 2004), pp. 79–93; Russell Hittinger, "Theology and Natural Law Theory," *Communio* (Fall 1990): pp. 402–408; Hittinger, *The First Grace*, pp. 3–37 (which is the first chapter of the book, titled: "Natural Law and Catholic Moral Theology"); Jacques Maritain, *Natural Law: Reflections on Theory and Practice* (South Bend, IN: St. Augustine's Press, 2001), pp. 25–38 (which is the second chapter of the book, titled: "The Ontological and Epistemological Elements of Natural Law").

Although Farrell does not use the word "teleology" in *The Natural Law According to Aquinas and Suárez*, he repeatedly emphasizes the importance of the "end" (*finis*) and "the principle of finality" in natural law considerations.[11] As the "cause of all causes," the end, particularly, shapes all practical and moral questions and inquiries. And this is supremely true in the ethical and moral theory of Thomas Aquinas.

**1. Natural Law Teleology in Aquinas.**

(A) NATURAL INTENTION, INCLINATION, AND *PER SE* DETERMINATION. In the intricate prologue to his commentary on Saint John's Gospel, Aquinas adumbrates the way some attain "a knowledge of God himself through authority":

> Some people arrived at a knowledge of God himself through authority, and this is the most efficacious way. For we see natural things [*ea quae sunt in rebus naturalibus*] acting on account of an end and attaining useful and certain ends. And since they lack understanding, they are not able to direct themselves, but must be directed and moved through understanding [*per intellectum*] by another director. And hence it is that the motion of natural things to a certain end indicates the existence of something higher by which natural things are directed to an end and governed. And therefore, since the whole course of nature proceeds and is directed to an end in an orderly manner, we must posit something higher which directs and governs these things as Lord: and this is God.[12]

11. The word "end" appears one hundred and sixteen times in Farrell's text.

12. "Quidam enim per auctoritatem Dei in ipsius cognitionem pervenerunt; et haec est via efficacissima. Videmus enim ea quae sunt in rebus naturalibus,

A consideration of *teleology* mediates this approach to divine knowledge: "For we see things in nature acting on account of an *end*." Aquinas even claims that the observation and analysis of teleological order is the "most efficacious way" to theological cognition. The overarching influence of *end* is here considered under two aspects. First, Aquinas considers end vis-à-vis the *creature*. Second, he considers end vis-à-vis *God*. Aquinas notes that a fundamentally teleological orientation governs even those beings that "lack understanding." An absence of native active intelligence manifests itself (and results) in the inability of self-direction. Nonetheless, the presence of an end implies an intrinsic orientation and (even in the absence of *self*-direction) a *directedness* towards an end. In other words, the nature of an end still necessitates the contemporaneous presence of intellectuality in some form. The *de facto* orientation of non-self-directed-beings to an end attests to the existence of "something higher which directs and governs" even non-self-directed-beings. This "something higher" is God, the source both of contingent being and of its concurrent teleological orientation.

The importance of teleology even in natural beings (*in rebus naturalibus*) is difficult to overestimate.[13] The end is one of the

propter finem agere, et consequi utiles et certos fines; et cum intellectu careant, se ipsa dirigere non possunt, nisi ab aliquo dirigente per intellectum dirigantur et moveantur. Et hinc est quod ipse motus rerum naturalium in finem certum, indicat esse aliquid altius, quo naturales res diriguntur in finem et gubernantur. Et ideo cum totus cursus naturae ordinate in finem procedat et dirigatur, de necessitate oportet nos ponere aliquid altius, quod dirigat ista et sicut dominus gubernet: et hic est Deus" (*Super Evangelium S. Ioannis Lectura*, §3). Translation mine.

13. The universality of teleology—which extends even to natural beings—is a recurring theme in Aquinas's thought. For example, he makes the following comment in the second question of the *Summa Theologiae*: "For we see that

first principles of intelligibility in the orders of both being and action. If there were no final causality, there would be no active and formal principle.[14] Every act is only possible and intelligible vis-à-vis an end. Moreover, "in acting, every agent *intends an end*."[15] The Dominican commentator Francis Silvestri of Ferrara (Ferrariensis), in his commentary on *SCG* III, c. 2, §1, explains the logic behind this conclusion:

> The impetus [*impetus*] of every agent tends to something certain: sometimes to an action itself, sometimes to something done through the action. Therefore, every agent in acting intends an end—either the action [itself] when the action does not terminate in something done, or something done through the action, if something is effected through it.[16]

"Impetus" is the "actual inclination and motion of the agent," and this inclination terminates either in the *action itself* as end or in

anything which lacks cognition, namely, natural bodies, operate on account of an end" ("Videmus enim quod aliqua quae cognitione carent, scilicet corpora naturalia, operantur propter finem" [*ST* I, q. 2, a. 3]).

14. Cf. *SCG* III, c. 2, especially §3. Unless otherwise noted, all quotations from the five-volume English translation of the *Summa contra Gentiles* published by the University of Notre Dame Press in 1975 and translated with an introduction and notes by Anton C. Pegis, F.R.S.C., James F. Anderson, Charles J. O'Neill, and Vernon J. Bourke.

15. "Omne agens in agendo intendit aliquem finem" (*SCG* III, c. 2, §1). Emphasis added.

16. Commentary on *SCG* III, c. 2, §1: "Omnis agentis impetus ad aliquid certum tendit: quandoque qidem ad actionem ipsam; quandoque vero ad aliquid factum per actionum. Ergo omne agens in agendo intendit finem: aut actionem, quando actio non terminator ad aliquod factum; aut operatum per ipsam, si aliquid per ipsam efficiatur."

*something effected through the action* as end.[17] Acts only occur for the sake of an end, and acts arise from and manifest the nature of the agent (*agens*). As the *causa causarum*, the final cause exercises an influence upon contingent beings (at least) insofar as it shapes and directs their fundamental orientation and specifies their potency for natural fulfillment.[18]

Moreover, as Aquinas says in the *prooemium* to his commentary on Saint John's Gospel, the existence of order—even in the ontological constitution of natural beings—profoundly testifies to the presence of *divine intelligence* and the order it imparts in all created being: "Since the whole course of nature proceeds and is directed to an end in an orderly manner, we must posit something higher which directs and governs these things as Lord: and this is God."[19] Teleological order permeates all being. "Things that know their end are ordered to the end in the same way as things which do not know it."[20] God creates every contingent being (rational and non-rational).[21] God's providence extends to all of the beings he creates—he creates them exactly as providentially governed beings.[22] God's providence is

17. "Impetus, idest actualis inclinatio et motio, agentis" (ibid.). Emphasis in original.
18. "Nature as an active principle is a spontaneous source of purposeful activities, determined characteristics which are for the fulfillment of the individual" (James A. Weisheipl, O.P., *Nature and Motion in the Middle Ages*, ed. William E. Carroll [Washington, DC: The Catholic University of America Press, 1985], p. 25).
19. *Super Evangelium S. Ioannis Lectura*, no. 3.
20. *SCG* III, c. 2, §4.
21. "Every being in any way existing is from God" (*ST* I, q. 44, a. 1).
22. "For the same reason God is the ruler of things as He is their cause, because the same gives existence as gives perfection; and this belongs to government.... As there can be nothing which is not created by God, so there can be nothing which is not subject to His government" (*ST* I, q. 103, a. 5).

*per se* teleological.[23] And God's providential teleology extends even to the intrinsic ontological constitution of the beings he creates. Aquinas is adamant about this point, and he criticizes those who do not appreciate its truth and importance:

> He [Aristotle] rejects an external mover which would move these bodies *per se* after they obtained their specific form [*postquam sunt formam specificam sotita*]. For light things are indeed moved upward, and heavy bodies downward, *by the generator inasmuch as it gives them the form upon which such motion follows*, but they are moved *per accidens*, and not *per se*, by whatever removes an obstacle to their motion. However, some have claimed that after bodies of this kind have received their form, they need to be moved *per se* by something extrinsic. It is this claim that the Philosopher rejects here.[24]

23. "It is not fitting that the supreme goodness of God should produce things without giving them their perfection. Now a thing's ultimate perfection consists in the attainment of its end. Therefore it belongs to the Divine goodness, as it brought things into existence, so to lead them to their end: and this is to govern" (*ST* I, q. 103, a. 1). "In fact, to order to the end, to direct, is the very *ratio* of divine providence" (Oscar J. Brown, *Natural Rectitude and Divine Law in Aquinas* [Toronto: Pontifical Institute of Medieval Studies, 1981], p. 8).

24. *In I De caelo*, 18, §1. Emphasis added. Moreover, in his commentary on the *Physics*, Aquinas says: "In like manner, the one who casts down the pillar did not give the heavy object resting upon it the impetus or inclination to be downward, for it had that *from the first generator, which gave it the form upon which that inclination follows*" (*In VIII Phys.*, 8, §7). Emphasis added. Weisheipl concludes from these two passages of Aquinas's commentaries on the Aristotelian corpus that "the important point is that once a particular body is in existence, there is *no need* for an agent constantly acting upon it to account for its activity. The body itself *acts*" (*Nature and Motion*, p. 20). Emphasis in original.

Motion follows from the intrinsic principle of being: form. The educed form specifically constituting a natural being is its active and ordering principle. This motional order is rooted in the very nature of the being itself. Thus, the natural being is ordered to an end *per se*—through its nature and essence. And all of this arises from God's universal causality.

The recognition of divinely imparted teleological orientation in all contingent beings is the foundation for Aquinas's consideration of the natural law in the *Summa Theologiae*. Although Aquinas's articulation of natural law doctrine is well-known, explicit considerations of the natural law occur infrequently in the Thomistic corpus.[25] Aquinas's formal discussion of the natural law in the *Summa Theologiae* is quite discrete.[26] However, "natural law" as a *per se* teleological principle has a universally applicable, transcendental relevance to all of created reality in general and to human nature in particular. Considered under this formal aspect, the natural law (insofar as it is founded in the eternal law) is the foundation of the whole of Aquinas's theology. And to the extent that the science of theology is concerned with all beings (under theology's proper formal object), it is essentially and necessarily teleological.[27] Because all being is *per se* subject to the eternal law,

25. "Although Thomas Aquinas is rightly looked to as a major proponent of natural law...it is oddly true that there is only one place in the vast body of his writings where he engages in an extended and formal discussion of law and its various kinds" (Ralph McInerny, *Ethica Thomistica: The Moral Philosophy of Thomas Aquinas*, rev. ed. [Washington, DC: The Catholic University of America Press, 1997], p. 40).

26. *ST* I-II, q. 94.

27. Here we are considering the teleological nature of the *sacra doctrina* vis-à-vis the teleological nature of all beings as considered under the light of faith—the teleological order of natural beings is preserved even in their consideration within the *sacra doctrina*. However, it is worth noting that Aquinas

all being is teleologically constituted.[28] There are no "end-less" beings. Because all beings have a nature, they have a concurrent end. Thus, in a real intrinsic-natural sense, we can speak of all being (even non-rational, inanimate, natural beings) as possessing *final intentionality*. Of course, the use of "intention" is analogical. James A. Weisheipl, O.P., explains:

> This is not to say that inanimate beings have consciousness or knowledge of their aim. While it is true to say that such terms as "aim," "desire," "appetite," "intentionality," etc. are primarily used in the context of human activity, the *analogical* use of these terms with regard to inanimate movement does not mean to imply consciousness of aim in the bodies themselves. However, this aim does imply Supreme Intelligence which directs natural things.[29]

Weisheipl refers to this inherent ontological directedness as a being's "intrinsic intentionality of purpose."[30] "Every agent, both natural and voluntary, *intends an end* [*intendit finem*], though it does not follow that every agent knows the end [*cognoscat finem*] or deliberates about the end [*vel diliberet de*

also articulates the very form and origin (*quoad nos*) of the *sacra doctrina* in teleological terms: "It was necessary for man's salvation that there should be a knowledge revealed by God [*doctrinam quandam secundum revelationem divinam*]...because man is directed to God, as to an end [*sicut ad quendam finem*]" (*ST* I, q. 1, a. 1). The *sacra doctrina* arises out of a supernatural teleological orientation and this teleological orientation is the form that specifies the science (cf. *ST* I, q. 1, a. 2). Theology is formally teleological. See Thomas de Vio Cajetan's commentary on *ST* I, q. 1, a. 1.

28. *ST* I-II, q. 93, a. 1.
29. *Nature and Motion*, p. 22, n. 95. Emphasis in original.
30. Ibid., p. 26.

*fine*]."[31] Hence, properly speaking, intention is "pre-cognitive" and "pre-deliberative." The existence of a nature and the existence of an end are *per se* concurrent. Weisheipl adds: "'Nature' cannot be the source of mere activity, but it must primarily aim at some achievement acquired through movement." In other words, "just as all movement implies some 'aim,' the spontaneous source of movement necessarily has some aim in view."[32] Nature as "the spontaneous source of movement" is necessarily and *essentially* ordered to an end, even before it gives rise to actions ordered to an end.[33]

While *an end* is a prerequisite for teleological cognition and deliberation, *teleological cognition and deliberation* are emphatically *not* a prerequisite for the actual existence of a natural end. The end is first, *simpliciter*. If there is a nature, there is a natural end. This is an essential point within Aquinas's doctrine: *Teleology does not* per se *require cognition or deliberation.*[34] Teleological cognition and deliberation is appropriate to beings "whose actions are not determined" to specific ends (i.e., voluntary agents), because it is exactly through teleological cognition and deliberation that they determine their actions vis-à-vis an end. The end is, *per se* and by definition, the *motional term*. It *determines* the action.

31. *On the Principles of Nature*, c. 3. Unless otherwise noted, all quotations from *On the Principles of Nature* are taken from Ralph McInerny's translation in *Saint Thomas Aquinas: Selected Writings* (New York: Penguin Books, 1998), pp. 18–29. In this instance, however, McInerny's translation has been adjusted to reflect the literal sense of Aquinas's Latin.

32. Weisheipl, *Nature and Motion*, p. 22.

33. Weisheipl uses the word "spontaneous" to mean *intrinsic order of nature to an end* (cf. ibid., pp. 9–10).

34. Of course, here we are speaking of the cognition proper to contingent beings, not the *ratio* of God's eternal law.

However, in the case of purely "natural agents" (non-volitional), their actions are determined (*actiones determinatae*). Thus, "it is not necessary [for them] to choose [*eligere*] the things which are for the end [i.e., the 'means to the end,' *ea quae sunt ad finem*]."[35] Their teleological order to specific ends is *naturally predetermined.* Moreover, exactly as naturally determined towards certain ends, in the case of natural agency there are no possible varied means to the end. Because the nature of a natural being is concurrently constituted with a *per se* orientation to a determinate end, the means are naturally predetermined. The constitution of a natural being with a specific nature and its *per se* order to a determined end is the cause of the predetermination of the means. Such natural agency is *per se* ordered to an end. Such *per se* order is, by nature, non-variable and therefore non-deliberative. This non-deliberative teleological orientation arises because the nature itself is inner-determined to its end and its actions.[36]

Aquinas defends the intrinsic orientation of non-deliberative (i.e., natural) agency as authentically teleological by comparing it to voluntary agency: "since the voluntary agent, not the natural agent, deliberates, it can be argued that if a voluntary agent sometimes acts without deliberation then *a fortiori* the *natural agent can act for an end without deliberation.*"[37] He also maintains that

35. *On the Principles of Nature*, c. 3.

36. In his helpful commentary on Aquinas's *On the Principles of Nature*, Joseph Bobik summarizes Aquinas's teaching on this point: "A natural agent neither selects its end, nor chooses the means thereto. The actions of a natural agent are set or determined *by its nature*, just as, and because, *the ends which it pursues are determined by that same nature*" (*Aquinas on Matter and Form and the Elements: A Translation and Interpretation of the* De principiis naturae *and the* De mixtione elementorum *of St. Thomas Aquinas* [Notre Dame, IN: University of Notre Dame Press, 1998], p. 38). Emphasis added.

37. *On the Principles of Nature*, c. 3.

the teleological orientation of non-deliberative agency is authentically (albeit, analogically) *intentional*: "this intending [*hoc intendere*, i.e., the 'intending' of natural beings] is nothing other than the natural inclination [*naturalem inclinationem*] to something."[38] Here, Aquinas explicitly expresses *natural intention* as *inclination*. Inclination is foundationally a creature's *per se* (essential, pre-cognitional) intentional order to an end. "To say that a natural agent intends an end is simply to say that it has a natural inclination to perform the activities by which that end can be achieved."[39] We might also describe this "natural intention" or "natural inclination" as "physical intention" or "physical inclination" (insofar as the intention or inclination proceeds *per se* from the nature [*physis*] of the natural being).[40]

This distinction between the teleologies of natural agency and voluntary agency stems from the differing principles of their respective actions. "Every agent acts through *nature* [i.e., a natural agent] or through *intellect* [i.e., a voluntary agent]."[41] Both act for the sake of an end but in different ways: the voluntary agent's actions are not predetermined vis-à-vis the end (and therefore

38. Ibid.

39. "It is possible for a natural agent to intend an end without deliberating either about that end or about the means thereto" (Bobik, *Aquinas on Matter and Form and the Elements*, p. 39).

40. While Aquinas's exact terminology is generally preferable, we will occasionally employ the terms "physical intention" and "physical inclination" rather than "natural intention" or "natural inclination" in this essay in order to maintain consistent clarity regarding the subject of our terms: the *per se* teleological order stemming from a natural being's nature (*physis*) and not "natural" as opposed to "supernatural" or "graced."

41. "Omne agens vel agit per naturam, vel per intellectum" (*SCG* III, c. 2, §6). Translation mine (emphasis added). Of course, because the will is the rational appetite, the "intellectual agent" and the "volitional agent" are *secundum res* identical and will be regarded as synonymous for the purposes of this analysis.

deliberation about action is required), while the natural agent's actions are predetermined vis-à-vis the end (by its very nature, and therefore no deliberation is possible).

> Intellectual agents act for the sake of an end: they preconceive in their intellects that which occurs through the action; and they act from such preconception; this is to act through intellect. Just as the entire likeness of an effect [*tota similitudo effectus*] achieved by the actions of an *intelligent agent* exists in the intellect that preconceives it, so, too, does the likeness of a natural effect [*similitudo naturalis effectus*] pre-exist in the *natural agent*; and from this [*ex qua*] the action is determined to a definite effect [*ad hunc effectum determinatur*]. For fire generates [*generat*] fire, and an olive an olive. Therefore, as a [volitional] agent *through intellect* tends [*tendit*] to a determined end through his action, so does a [natural] agent *through its nature* [tend to a determined end]. Therefore, every agent acts for an end.[42]

The essential difference between volitional agents and natural agents is recognized in the intellectual *preconception* (*in intellectu*

42. "De agentibus autem per intellectum non est dubium quin agant propter finem: agunt enim praeconcipientes in intellectu id quod per actionem consequuntur, et ex tali praeconceptione agunt; hoc enim est agere per intellectum. Sicut autem in intellectu praeconcipiente existit tota similitudo effectus ad quem per actiones intelligentis pervenitur, ita in agente naturali praeexistit similitudo naturalis effectus, ex qua actio ad hunc effectum determinatur: nam ignis generat ignem, et oliva olivam. Sicut igitur agens per intellectum tendit in finem determinatum per suam actionem, ita agens per naturam. Omne igitur agens agit propter finem" (*SCG* III, c. 2, §6). Translation mine (emphasis added).

*praeconcipiente*) of the "entire likeness of the [action's] effect" in the intellect of the former, and in the natural *pre-existence* of the "likeness of the natural effect" (*praeexistit similitudo naturalis effectus*) in the nature of the latter (*in agente naturali*). Natural agents are *per se* determined and ordered to their effects. Thus, fire generates fire and not a cat; and an olive generates an olive tree and not a stone. Volitional agents are not *per se* ordered, and their determination is intellectual in origin—it is reached *per intellectum*; preconceiving the action and its effects vis-à-vis the end. The essential difference between volitional agency and natural agency is predicated upon this formal difference. The actional form of the volitional agent is an *intellectually preconceived* similitude of order to an end. The actional form of the natural agent, however, is the *inclination of the natural form itself* to an end. Sylvester Ferrariensis explains the *formal* origin of the difference between intellectual intention and physical inclination:

> The end [*ultimum*] that the natural agent intends through its action is *the likeness of form* through which it acts; as the end [*ultimum*] that an agent [i.e., a volitional agent] intends through the intellect is that to which he is assimilated through his preconception. The impetus of an agent [i.e., a natural agent] follows *the inclination of the form* through which it operates.[43]

43. "Ultimum enim quod per suam actionem intendit agens naturale, est similitudo formae per quam agit; sicut ultimum quod intendit agens per intellectum, est id cui per suam praeconceptionem assimilatur: impetus enim agentis sequitur inclinationem formae per quam operatur" (Commentary on *SCG* III, c. 2, §5). Emphasis added.

Their intrinsic teleological constitution explains why natural beings are ordered to their end *per se*. An intellectual preconception of an actional form is not a necessary precondition for the execution of their proper actions. Rather, their natural form is *itself* the *pre-existent* principle of their proper action. The actional effect flows directly and essentially from its nature. Thus, natural agents are *per se* determined and ordered to their effects.

The *per se* determination and order of natural agency is essentially foundational to Aquinas's account of teleology. Metaphysically, it is the most basic and fundamental instance of teleological order in contingent reality. The entirety of his teleological doctrine is dependent upon this most fundamental increment of being: the *per se* order and determination of natural agency.

(B) Inclination, intention, and teleology as law. The very first article of Aquinas's consideration of the extrinsic principles of human action in the *Summa Theologiae* raises the question: "Whether law is something pertaining to reason?"[44] This question educes a principle of vital significance for his subsequent legal discussions in general and for his natural law inquiries in particular. Aquinas begins his response by observing that the imperative nature of "law" necessitates its grounding in reason.[45] "Law is a rule and measure of acts, whereby man is induced to act or restrained from acting." The necessary rational form of all law arises from the radical priority of the *end* as the first principle of all action: "every agent, of necessity, acts for an end."[46] The

44. *ST* I-II q. 90, a. 1.

45. Cf. *ST* I-II q. 90, a. 1, *sed contra.*

46. *ST* I-II q. 1, a. 2.

nature of law—ruling and measuring human acts—is rational because human acts are ordered to an end, and "it belongs to the reason to direct to the end."[47] There is no agent or action without an end. Additionally, (practical) reason *orders* to an end.[48] As an "end-less" being and an "end-less" action are *per se* unintelligible, so an authentically "end-less" order is *per se* unintelligible—true order is always ordered *to* something (the end). The end gives rise to and specifies authentic order. It belongs to reason to grasp or impart this order. Therefore the *ratio* of law (as a principle of order) pertains to reason.

Aquinas explains that the ruling, measuring, and therefore ordering nature of law can exist in something in two ways.[49] First, the principle of ruling and measuring can be found in the *measurer* or *ruler* (*sicut in mensurante et regulante*). Considered under this aspect, "law is in reason alone." However, there is a second aspect of law: The principle of ruling and measuring can also reside in the *recipient* of the law, in that which is *ruled* and *measured* (*sicut in regulato et mensurato*). Here, Aquinas explains that this reception of ordering principles establishes *inclination as law*: "law is in all those things that are inclined [*inclinatur*] to something by reason of some law."[50] The law of inclination is thus *a passive constitution in teleological order*. Hence, while the law of inclination may be pre-cognitive and pre-deliberative vis-à-vis the passive subject (as in the case of natural beings), it is not non-cognitive *simpliciter*. If

47. *ST* I-II, q. 90, a. 1.

48. "Rationis enim est ordinare ad finem" (*ST* I-II q. 90, a. 1). Cf. *ST* I-II q. 91, a. 1: "A law is nothing else but a dictate of *practical reason* emanating from the ruler who governs a perfect community." Emphasis added.

49. *ST* I-II, q. 90, a. 1, ad 1.

50. Ibid.

the law of inclination is a truly inclinative—and therefore, reflects order to an end—then intelligence is present at least in the extrinsic source of the passively constituted teleological order of any real being. The law of inclination receives its (even purely natural) normativity from a teleological order that presupposes reason. All beings are inclined to—and (at least physically) intend—an end. Not all beings possess reason. However, the presence of true inclination presupposes and requires intelligence and cognition. Thus, technically speaking, the law of inclination is truly legal by way of analogy. Aquinas concludes: "any inclination [*inclinatio*] arising from a law may be called law, not essentially, but by participation as it were."[51] In his article examining the cause of law, Aquinas re-emphasizes the participative nature of law in the recipient of the order imposed: "A law is in a person not only as in one that rules, but also by participation as in one that is ruled. In the latter way each one is a law to himself, insofar as he shares the direction that he receives from the one who rules him."[52] Again, this resonates with Weisheipl's observation that while "end" or "aim" and "intentionality" "are primarily used in the context of human activity, the *analogical* use of these terms with regard to inanimate movement" is speculatively justified.[53] Although Aquinas is formally speaking about the inclination of law pertaining to humans in *ST* I-II, q. 90, a. 1, ad 1, his reference

51. "Et sic lex est in omnibus quae inclinantur in aliquid ex aliqua lege, ita quod quaelibet inclinatio proveniens ex aliqua lege, potest dici lex, non essentialiter, sed quasi participative" (ibid.).

52. *ST* I-II, q. 90, a. 3, ad 1. This participative aspect of the legal order of God is explicitly connected to the eternal law: "every knowledge of truth is a kind of reflection and participation of the eternal law, which is the unchangeable truth" (*ST* I-II, q. 93, a. 2).

53. Weisheipl, *Nature and Motion*, p. 22, n. 95.

to the intellectual foundations of real inclination is legitimately applicable to all instances of inclination (even to the inclination of natural beings).[54] Intelligence is the foundation for all inclination—even if the intelligence is only the "Supreme Intelligence."

After his preliminary analysis of inclination under the *ratio* of law, Aquinas offers a summary of the different kinds of laws. The first and foundational type of law he describes is the *eternal law*.[55] Aquinas maintains the critical importance and foundational relevance of the eternal law to all further speculative inquiries.[56] The eternal law is the common denominator of all theological considerations of created being. The reason for this is simple: The eternal law is itself the ontological "dictate" (*dictamen*) flowing from God's divine knowledge and providence.[57] All things are subject to his providence.[58] Providence is nothing other than the "reason of order" (*ratio ordinis*); and the execution of reasoned order is government (*gubernatio*). The former is eternal, the latter temporal.[59] Thus, the eternal law is God's reason, his divine knowledge—his "eternal concept" of reality.[60] Put otherwise, the eternal law is nothing less than *how God knows*

54. Farrell observes that "by the natural inclinations this law is brought into relation with the natural physical laws; by the proposition of reason and the light of reason which it presupposes, it is lifted to heights peculiar to man, i.e., to the moral field" (*Natural Law According to Aquinas and Suárez*, p. 102).

55. *ST* I-II, q. 91, a. 1; *ST* I-II, q. 93.

56. Cf. *ST* I-II, q. 93, a. 2.

57. Cf. *ST* I-II, q. 91, a. 3, ad 1. For an interesting interpretation of the eternal law in the thought of St. Thomas Aquinas, see John Rziha, *Perfecting Human Actions: St. Thomas Aquinas on Human Participation in Eternal Law* (Washington, DC: The Catholic University of America Press, 2009).

58. Cf. *ST* I, q. 22, a. 2.

59. *ST* I, q. 22, a. 1, ad 2.

60. Cf. *ST* I-II, q. 91, a. 1.

*the world to be.*[61] Aquinas explains: "Just as in every artificer there pre-exists a type [*ratio*] of the things that are made by his art, so too in every governor there must pre-exist the type [*ratio*] of the order of those things that are to be done by those who are subject to his government."[62] This rational type pre-existing in the one who governs "bears the character of law [*rationem legis obtinet*]."[63] God as creator stands in relation to the things he creates "as the artificer to the products of his art."[64] Moreover, God "governs all the acts and movements that are to be found in each single creature."[65] Thus, the *ratio* of the divine wisdom (*ratio divine sapientiae*) has a twofold nature: "inasmuch as by it all things are created, [the *ratio*] has the character of art, exemplar or idea…so as *moving all things to their due ends*, [the *ratio*] bears the character of law." Aquinas therefore concludes: "The eternal law is nothing else than the type of divine wisdom, as directing all actions and movements."[66]

The providential, governmental order that flows from the eternal wisdom of God is deeply integrated into the very nature of contingent being. "God imprints [*imprimit*] on the whole of nature the principles of its proper actions. And so, in this way, God is said to command the whole of nature."[67] Contingent being

61. Romanus Cessario, O.P., expresses it thus: "Eternal law represents how God knows the world to be, how he effectively conceives the ordering of everything that exists within creation" (*Introduction to Moral Theology*, rev. ed. [Washington, DC: The Catholic University of America Press, 2013], pp. 56–57). See also Brown, *Natural Rectitude and Divine Law in Aquinas*, pp. 1–12.

62. *ST* I-II, q. 93, a. 1.

63. Ibid.

64. Ibid. Cf. *ST* I, q. 14, a. 8.

65. Ibid. Cf. *ST* I, q. 103, a. 5.

66. Ibid.

67. *ST* I-II, q. 93, a. 5.

and the order proper to it are, by nature, created. This universal impress of the *ratio* of divine wisdom on all being (in appropriate proportion) is how the eternal law is duly promulgated: "the impression of an inward active principle is to natural things, what the promulgation of law is to men."[68] Moreover creation and its contingent order are concurrent realities. Every creature, rational and not, is subject to the teleological order imprinted by the divine wisdom. "Irrational creatures are subject to the eternal law, through being moved by divine providence; but not, as rational creatures are, *through understanding the divine commandment*."[69] The eternal law thus affords the theologian the *ratio* for why a created, contingent being is what it is and is not what it is not; and, concurrently, its due (and, derivatively, its undue) order. The eternal law assures the theologian that every created being is the recipient of a natural, intrinsic order that flows from the divine knowledge of the contingent being.[70] In short: A being is as God

68. *ST* I-II, q. 90, a. 5. Farrell highlights this point: "In subjecting these natural things to the Eternal Law, St. Thomas is using the term 'law' in a broad analogical sense for the purpose of indicating that everything is subject to divine direction. A human legislator by his precept imprints something, so to speak, on the mind of his subjects which is the principle of action of these subjects as such, that is the '*verbum mentale*' is imprinted on the minds of men as the result of the promulgation of the law. In governing the world, God imprints on the whole of creation the natural principles which govern the proper actions of every individual nature" (*Natural Law According to Aquinas and Suárez*, p. 46).

69. Ibid. Emphasis added.

70. Aquinas also offers a significant account of how the *ratio* of the divine wisdom is different from the *ratio* of human knowledge of created being: "The types [*ratio*] of the divine intellect do not stand in the same relation to things, as the types of the human intellect. For the human intellect is measured by things, so that a human concept is not true by reason of itself, but by reason of its being consonant with things, since 'an opinion is true or false according as it answers to the reality.' But the divine intellect is the measure of things: since each thing has so far truth in it, as it represents the divine intellect, as was stated

knows it to be, and, subsequently, it is ordered to the end to which he knows it to be ordered. "The law denotes a kind of plan [*ratio*] directing acts towards an end."[71] The ordering *ratio* of law is *per se* teleological. While one can recognize by reason alone this teleological law of inclination proper to natural beings, it assumes deeper meaning when considered under the light of faith. The law of inclination becomes more pellucid the more one becomes aware of its *per se* relation to the "Supreme Intelligence, Measurer, and Ruler" that constitutes the teleological order. The consideration of the law of inclination moves from a formally philosophical analysis into that of a formally theological analysis when the law of inclination is considered vis-à-vis a divinely revealed *Law Giver*. Aquinas considers the eternal and the natural law under this properly *theological* aspect in the *Summa Theologiae*.[72]

Aquinas's understanding of the eternal law informs his teaching on the natural law. Because of their shared foundation in the law of inclination, there is profound harmony between the eternal law and the natural law.[73] In fact, Aquinas himself concedes

---

in *ST* I, q. 16, a. 1. Consequently the divine intellect is true in itself; and its type is truth itself" (*ST* I-II, q. 93, a. 1, ad 3). While the *ratio* of the divine intellect stands as active principle towards the things created—as *measuring* principle—the *ratio* of the human intellect stands as passive principle towards the essences God creates. The *ratio* of the human intellect is formally *measured* by the *ratio* of the divine intellect.

71. *ST* I-II, q. 93, a. 3.

72. Cf. Cessario, "Why Aquinas Locates the Natural Law within the *Sacra Doctrina*," pp. 79–93; Fulvio Di Blasi, *God and the Natural Law: A Rereading of Thomas Aquinas*, trans. David Thunder (South Bend, IN: St. Augustine's Press, 2006).

73. Matthew Levering states the point this way: "[The natural law is] not a rationalistic rulebook, but the eternal law imprinted in the spiritual-bodily human person, who participates rationally in God's teleological ordering of the human beings to their fulfillment" (*Biblical Natural Law: A Theocentric and Teleological Approach* [Oxford: Oxford University Press, 2008], p. 21).

(slightly) to those who object that there is no need for the natural law because "man is sufficiently governed" by the eternal law.[74] He admits that the governance of the eternal law is indeed sufficient in and of itself. However, Aquinas reminds his interlocutor that the natural law is nothing other than a *rational participation* in this same eternal law, because "the first direction of our acts to their end [by way of reason and will] must needs be in virtue of the natural law."[75] He offers the following explanation:

> Hence, since all things which are subject to divine providence are ruled and measured by the eternal law...it is manifest that all things participate in some way [*aliqualiter*] in the eternal law insofar, namely, as they have from its impression inclinations to proper acts and ends [*ex impressione eius habent inclinationes in proprios actus et fines*]. Among the other creatures, however, the rational creature is subject to divine providence in a more excellent mode, insofar as he becomes a participant in providence, providing for himself and for others. Wherefore he also participates in the eternal reason [*ratio aeterna*] itself, through which he has a natural inclination to his due act and end [*per quam habet naturalem inclinationem ad debitum actum et finem*]. And such a participation of the eternal law in a rational creature is called the natural law.[76]

74. *ST* I-II, q. 91, a. 2, obj. 1.
75. *ST* I-II, q. 91, a. 2, ad 2.
76. "Unde cum omnia quae divinae providentiae subduntur, a lege aeterna regulentur et mensurentur, ut ex dictis patet; manifestum est quod omnia participant aliqualiter legem aeternam, inquantum scilicet ex impressione eius habent inclinationes in proprios actus et fines. Inter cetera autem rationalis

This passage from the *Summa Theologiae* is speculatively rich and entails many implications on the level of nature as well as on the level of grace. All creatures have received the law of inclination through the impress of the *ratio* of God's wisdom. In this way, all creatures participate in the very *ratio* of God. However, non-rational and rational creatures have received this impress in a way proper to their natures. In human creatures, the *impressio* of the divine eternal law results in the rationally informed inclinations proper to the human person. This rationally qualified participation in the divine reason is the specific difference between the eternal and the natural law (and between the participation of natural beings and rational beings in the teleological law of inclination). Aquinas accentuates this point in his response to a later objection when he states that "even irrational animals participate in the eternal reason according to their own mode, just as the rational creature." However, "the rational creature participates in it intellectually and rationally," and thus "the participation of the eternal law in the rational creature is properly called a law."[77]

The order proper to law in both its passive and active aspects is most fully reflected in those who themselves can grasp the principle of order. While all beings passively participate in the teleological law of inclination, only rational beings can *formally*

creatura excellentiori quodam modo divinae providentiae subiacet, inquantum et ipsa fit providentiae particeps, sibi ipsi et aliis providens. Unde et in ipsa participatur ratio aeterna, per quam habet naturalem inclinationem ad debitum actum et finem. Et talis participatio legis aeternae in rationali creatura lex naturalis dicitur" (*ST* I-II, q. 91, a. 2).

77. "Ad tertium dicendum quod etiam animalia irrationalia participant rationem aeternam suo modo, sicut et rationalis creatura. Sed quia rationalis creatura participat eam intellectualiter et rationaliter, ideo participatio legis aeternae in creatura rationali proprie lex vocatur " (*ST* I-II, q. 91, a. 2, ad 3).

participate in this law *as law*. This is clearly the case because only rational creatures can receive the *ratio* of the divine wisdom in a properly *rational* manner and under a *rational* aspect. The human creature's unique participation in the eternal law is rational because the human creature can formally (albeit, partially) comprehend the *ratio* of the divine wisdom. Intelligence—and its power to discern and impart order to an end—is the prerequisite of law. While natural beings only participate in the ordering intelligence passively through physical inclination, rational beings are able to participate in this ordering intelligence *both* passively (the universal law of inclination) *and* actively (through intellect and will). "To the natural law belongs those things to which a man is inclined naturally: and among these it is proper to man to be inclined to act according to reason."[78]

Essential to Aquinas's theology in general—and to his natural law doctrine in particular—is the fact that the active participation of rational creatures in the eternal law presupposes and is built upon the creature's passive participation in the eternal law. It is only because of a creature's constitutional *reception* of the teleological order of God's *aeterna ratio* that it is able to participate rationally in this same ordering. As we observed earlier: the *end* is a prerequisite for teleological cognition and deliberation, philosophical or theological. However, the *teleological cognition and deliberation* of the rational creature are emphatically *not* a prerequisite for the actual existence of authentic teleological order. The law of inclination to an end is first, *simpliciter et universaliter*. All creatures—natural and rational—participate in the eternal law's inclinative ordering. This is an essential point within Aquinas's

78. *ST* I-II, q. 94, a. 4.

theological doctrine regarding the natural law: *Teleology—whether it be considered under philosophical or theological aspects—does not* per se *follow the recipient's subjective cognition and deliberation.* Indeed, the rational creature's participation (*as rational*) in the eternal law requires the pre-cognitional and pre-deliberative establishment of the teleological law of inclination.[79] By definition, all beings possess a nature *per se* ordered to an end. There are no end-less beings, rational or otherwise.

## II. Natural Law Teleology in *Veritatis Splendor*

The historic encyclical *Veritatis Splendor* was promulgated in 1993.[80] Pope John Paul II formulates its purpose around the necessity of reflecting upon "the whole of the Church's moral teaching, with the precise goal of recalling certain fundamental truths of Catholic doctrine."[81] In a word, the encyclical seeks to rearticulate the Church's teaching about the moral life according to its proper "theological nature."[82] This focus emerges in large part because of a "lack of harmony between the traditional response of the

79. Steven A. Long summarizes this point with helpful precision: "The creature's passive participation in the eternal law is the precondition for the active, rational, and preceptive participation that is the natural law, as well as the condition for the specific obediential potency for grace" ("Speculative Foundations of Moral Theology and the Causality of Grace," *Studies in Christian Ethics*, Vol. 23, No. 4 (2010): pp. 397–414 [p. 413]).

80. For two, fundamentally different, considerations of *Veritatis Splendor*, see Michael E. Allsopp and John J. O'Keefe, eds., *Veritatis Splendor: American Responses* (Kansas City, MO: Sheed and Ward, 1995); and J. A. Di Noia, O.P., and Romanus Cessario, O.P., ed., *Veritatis Splendor and the Renewal of Moral Theology* (Princeton, NJ: Scepter Publishers, 1999).

81. Pope John Paul II, *Veritatis Splendor* [*The Splendor of the Truth*] (1993), §4.

82. Ibid.

Church and certain theological positions, encountered even in Seminaries and Faculties of Theology."[83]

> The specific purpose of the present Encyclical is this: to set forth, with regard to the problems being discussed, the principles of moral teaching based upon Sacred Scripture and the living Apostolic Tradition, and at the same time to shed light on the presuppositions and consequences of the dissent which that teaching has met.[84]

The encyclical frequently repeats the fundamental point that "only God can answer the question about what is good, because he is the Good itself."[85] The Church teaches (following the example of our Lord himself) that she always brings the question of goodness—particularly moral goodness—"back to its religious foundations."[86] Thus the *per se* theological nature of the question of moral goodness emerges clearly and early in the teaching of the encyclical.[87] The significance of this theocentric foundation of the moral teaching of the Church is recognized when one understands that "the moral life presents itself as the response due to the many gratuitous initiatives taken by God out of love for man."[88] The moral life is the human response to the divine initiative on

83. Ibid.
84. Ibid., §5.
85. Ibid., §9. "Only God can answer the question about the good, because he is the Good" (§12).
86. Ibid.
87. "What man is and what he must do becomes clear as soon as God reveals himself" (ibid., §10).
88. Ibid.

the order of nature and on the order of grace. The centrality of the divine initiative runs throughout the Church's considerations of moral truth on both the natural and supernatural levels. God's initiation is an integral part to the ontological-moral fabric of all of reality. "God has already given an answer to this question [about the identity of the good]: he did so *by creating man and ordering him* with wisdom and love to his final end, through the law which is inscribed in his heart (cf. *Rom.* 2:15), the 'natural law.'"[89]

*Veritatis Splendor* identifies the divine answer to the question as "already" present and given—indeed, imparted—in the natural law. The natural law is, as it were, the primordial answer to the question about human goodness and the perfective fulfillment that the divine order extends to the human order.[90] The question of moral goodness receives its existence and its subsequent intelligibility through its created nature and the relevant order which is necessarily concurrent with such creation. The existence and the order of man proceeds from God's own divine wisdom and love. Moreover, this wisdom and love constitute man in a created order established formally with a particular *final end.* Teleology is a constitutive element of the human person, and it is present even within the most intrinsic and inherent recesses of the human nature. The natural order is permeated with teleology.

89. Ibid., §12.

90. "But if God alone is the Good, no human effort, not even the most rigorous observances of the commandments, succeeds in 'fulfilling' the Law, that is, acknowledging the Lord as God and rendering him the worship due to him alone (cf. *Mt.* 4:10). *This 'fulfillment' can come only from a gift of God*: the offer of a share in the divine goodness revealed and communicated in Jesus, the one whom the rich young man addresses with the words 'Good Teacher'" (ibid., §11). Emphasis in original.

This wise and loving order receives specific denomination within the title "natural law." The natural law is, simply, the teleological order flowing from God's wisdom and love. The intelligible *ratio* which the human intellect perceives within created reality is the "rational—and thus universally understandable and communicable—character of the moral norms belonging to the sphere of the natural moral law."[91] The encyclical reasserts "the fact that the natural moral law has God as its author, and that man, by the use of reason, participates in the eternal law, which is not for him to establish."[92]

The divine and therefore revealed tenor of this ordering receives concrete expression in and through the precepts of the Decalogue. *Veritatis Splendor* cites Aquinas's sermons on the Decalogue for clarification about the nature of the natural law: "[The natural law] is nothing other than the light of understanding infused in us by God, whereby we understand what must be done and what must be avoided. God gave this light and this law to man at creation."[93] The encyclical adverts to the moral "centrality of the Decalogue," because every precept contained therein is an interpretation and application of "what the words 'I am the Lord your God' mean for man."[94] Indeed, "the different commandments of the Decalogue are really only so many reflections of the one commandment about the good of the person, at the level of

91. Ibid., §36.

92. Ibid.

93. Ibid., §12. Saint Thomas Aquinas, *In duo praecepta caritatis et in cecem legis praecepta. Prologus: Opuscula theologica*, II, No. 1129, ed. Taurinen (1954), p. 245. *Veritatis Splendor* also points to resonances of this teaching in *ST* I-II, q. 91, a. 2 and the *Catechism of the Catholic Church*, 2nd ed. (Città del Vaticano: Libreria Editrice Vaticana, 1997), §1955.

94. *Veritatis Splendor*, §13.

the many different goods which characterize his identity as a spiritual and bodily being in relationship with God, with his neighbor and with the material world."[95] Here goodness—particularly, the human good—stands as centrally important and theocentrically founded: "The commandments of which Jesus reminds the young man are meant to safeguard *the good* of the person, the image of God, by protecting his *goods*."[96] The encyclical adverts to the various remotions of goodness. The goodness of the person receives its objective nature from its correlation to the *imago Dei*.

Moreover, the good of the person is also related to the proper order which the moral agent ought to preserve and instill in external *goods*. Thus, goodness receives its full expression even amidst its broad diversity. The commandments "bear witness to the fundamental relationship between freedom and divine law." *Veritatis Splendor* emphatically teaches that "human freedom and God's law are not in opposition; on the contrary, they appeal one to the other."[97] In short, the moral agent must not forget about "the fundamental dependence of freedom upon truth."[98] "God's plan poses no threat to man's genuine freedom; on the contrary, the acceptance of God's plan is the only way to affirm that freedom."[99]

The first explicit reference to the natural law in the document appears within an examination of human freedom and moral truth. The encyclical observes the modern penchant for "detaching human freedom from its essential and constitutive relationship

95. Ibid.

96. Ibid. Emphasis in original.

97. Ibid., §17.

98. Ibid., §34.

99. Ibid., §45.

to truth." Because of this deleterious detachment, "the traditional doctrine regarding the natural law, and the universality and the permanent validity of its precepts is rejected."[100] This analysis of the natural law is quite significant. The encyclical, in effect, argues that a robust account of the natural law plays an integral part of the unity between human freedom and moral truth. Moral truth and moral freedom presuppose and require the natural law. How can this be? Initially, the existentially complex dynamism between freedom and truth appears to be only *per accidens* related to the Church's teaching on the natural law. On the contrary, however, the encyclical argues that there exists a far more *immanent* and *intrinsic* connection between human freedom and moral truth precisely within their natural law foundation: The natural law is an integral part of the synergistic nature of human freedom and moral truth.

*Veritatis Splendor* observes that "this law is called natural law…not because it refers to the nature of irrational beings but because the reason which promulgates it is proper to human nature."[101] Nonetheless, this rational foundation identifies as its source "the divine wisdom as moving all things to their due end."[102] The encyclical summarizes these themes under the heading "theonomy": "Others speak, and rightly so, of *theonomy*, or *participated theonomy*, since man's free obedience to God's law effectively implies that human reason and human will participate in God's wisdom and providence."[103] Citing the Second Vatican

100. Ibid., §4.
101. Ibid., §44.
102. Ibid., §43; citing *ST* I-II, q. 93, a. 1.
103. Ibid., §41. Emphasis in original.

Council, the encyclical explicitly references the teleological nature of the eternal law and, derivatively, of the natural law.[104] The eternal law is divine providence, "a love which cares."[105] Moreover, this loving, providential care, affects man "not 'from without,' through the laws of physical nature, but 'from within,' through reason, which, by its natural knowledge of God's eternal law, is consequently able to show man the right direction to take in his free actions."[106] The natural law is realized through man's rational participation in the intrinsic, impressed ordering of the eternal law. "The natural law enters here as the human expression of God's eternal law."[107] The human person *expresses* the ordering *ratio* of God which has been *impressed*; and thus, this human expression of the order of the eternal law is *per se* teleological. *Veritatis Splendor* is unambiguous regarding the teleological nature of this order: It is through "a natural inclination to its proper act and end" that the rational creature shares in "the Eternal Reason" itself.[108] Hence, the natural law emerges as a teleological unity because of its rational conformity to the eternal reason of God. "It follows that the natural law is *itself the eternal law*, implanted in beings endowed with reason, and inclining them *towards their right action and end*; it is none other than the eternal reason of the Creator and Ruler of the universe."[109]

104. "The Council refers back to the classic teaching on *God's eternal law*" (ibid., §43). Emphasis in original. *Veritatis Splendor* is here referring to *Dignitatis Humanae* [Declaration on Religious Freedom] (1965), §3.

105. *Veritatis Splendor*, §43.

106. Ibid. Here the encyclical cites *ST* I-II, q. 90, a. 4, ad 1.

107. Ibid.

108. Ibid.

109. Ibid., §44; citing Leo XIII, *Libertas Praestantissimum* [On the Nature of Human Liberty] (1888), §219. Emphasis in original.

The encyclical observes that some ethicists "can be tempted to take as the standard for their discipline and even for its operative norms the result of a statistical study of concrete human behavior patterns and the opinions about morality encountered in the majority of people." Moreover, other moralists "conceive of freedom as somehow in opposition to or in conflict with material and biological nature." Both positions ultimately rely upon a moral analysis which is fundamentally extrinsic to the reality of the human person; and, thus, they are ultimately unsatisfying because they do not conform to the truth of the eternal law (which is intrinsic). *Veritatis Splendor* diagnoses the shared malady at the root of both errors: "Here various approaches are at one in overlooking the *created dimension of nature and in misunderstanding its integrity*."[110] "For some, 'nature' becomes reduced to raw material for human activity and for its power." This conceptualization reduces nature to the level of a pure *privation* of human freedom—"inasmuch as it represents a limitation and denial of [due] freedom."[111] "For others...nature would thus come to mean everything found in man and the world apart from freedom."[112] Here nature (seen over and against human freedom) is reduced to a *pure passive potency*, and would thus "be reduced to and treated as a readily available biological or social material."[113] A radical conception of human autonomy that is inimical to the teleological order of human nature is not adequately proportioned to the Church's understanding of the moral life. Such a conception of

110. Ibid., §46. Emphasis added.

111. Ibid.

112. Ibid.

113. Cf. Ibid., §48.

absolute human autonomy fails to consider the truth of the eternal law as it is impressed upon all contingent being, and thus occasions two fundamental moral errors. The conclusion both errors necessitate is unsatisfying: "When all is said and done man would not even have a nature; he would be his own personal life-project. Man would be nothing more than his own freedom."[114] This conclusion does not attain the fully satisfying position because it separates the unity between authentic freedom and moral truth that the encyclical is expressly intent on maintaining.

There is an *immanent* and *intrinsic* connection between human freedom and moral truth precisely within the natural law constitution of the human person. The natural law does not admit to any "division between freedom and nature."[115] *Veritatis Splendor* states that "since man's free obedience to God's law effectively implies that human reason and will participate in God's wisdom and providence" some theologians have "rightly" classified these themes under the heading of *theonomy* or *participated theonomy.*[116] Theonomy thus encompasses the inclinative ordering of God's impressed wisdom but under a formally theological aspect.

## III. From Natural Teleology to Natural Law Teleology

Every being has a nature, *per se.* Every nature has an end, *per se.* Therefore, every being has an end, *per se.* All being is thus formally and necessarily teleological in essential constitution. There are no

114. Ibid., §46.

115. Ibid., §50.

116. Cf. Cessario, *Introduction to Moral Theology*, pp. 215–18.

"end-less" beings. Because all beings have a nature, they have a necessarily concurrent end. Moreover, there are no "end-less" motions or actions. Motions and actions are only intelligible vis-à-vis an end, elsewise the motions and actions would have no intelligible reason for beginning and no terminative point of conclusion. Finally, there is no such thing as an "end-less" order. The end gives rise to and specifies authentic order; and it belongs to reason to grasp and impart the due priority and posteriority proper to order. The teleology of final causality carries universal significance and relevance within any consideration of being.

*Natural teleology* becomes *natural law teleology* when the natural teleology is assumed by *reason*. Thus Aquinas defines the "natural law" as the rational creature's participation in the eternal law. Only the rational creature is able to participate in the eternal *ratio* of God under the formal aspect of *ratio*. Additionally, the rational creature is able to grasp aspects of God's eternal law as formally *God's*. Thus *Veritatis Splendor* and others describe the human participation in God's eternal law as properly "theonomic." Through his reason, man is able to recognize the formal integrity of the eternal law of God as both *theological* (because of its divine establishment) and *legal* (because of its essential teleological constitution). Understanding the teleological order proper to law requires rationality. Understanding God's eternal law as *law* and as *God's* requires rationality. Once the full *ratio-nal* dimension of the eternal law of God is recognized, the eternal law can be accurately described in the knowing subject as *the natural law*.[117] It is

117. For a further development of this theme, see Stephen L. Brock, "The Legal Character of Natural Law According to St. Thomas Aquinas" (PhD diss., University of Toronto, 1988).

through this formally rational comprehension that the eternal law is the natural law. For through this comprehension, the rational creature is able not merely to participate *passively* in the law of inclination the eternal wisdom of God impresses on all contingent being, the rational creature is also able to participate *actively* in this teleological order under a formally teleological aspect. Teleology, order, and rationality are all self-referential and mutually presuppositive (even in their merely passive instantiations). Thus, the rational creature alone can grasp their interdependence and conjoined integrity. Only the rational creature's participation in the eternal law is properly natural law because he alone grasps the full natural *ratio-nal* saturation of the eternal law in all of its natural impressions.

However, even when reason understands the intrinsic teleology of the natural order, the law of inclination proper to natural teleology *still remains*. The passive participation of all creatures (non-rational and rational) in the eternal law is the essential precondition for the rational creature's active participation in the eternal law. The fundamental law of inclination universal to all contingent being is not forfeited through the rational knowledge of the law of inclination. The universal law of the eternal *ratio* absolutely precedes the natural law proper to rational creatures. The rational creature's participation in the eternal law is dependent upon the prior teleological constitution of all created reality.

* * *

Farrell remarks that "the best expression of the aim of this dissertation would be to say it hopes to bring out some of the intellectual treasures that St. Thomas put into his profound definitions and explanations of law, the Eternal Law and the Natural Moral Law."[118] He certainly did not think that his was the final word on these matters. And whether he adequately achieved his goal remains a separate question. Many valuable studies of Aquinas's natural law doctrine have appeared after the original 1930 publication of *The Natural Law According to Aquinas and Suárez*, and still more will follow. Nonetheless, this early text from Farrell's pen remains a valuable resource for natural lawyers in general and students of Aquinas in particular. Why? Although it was published some fifty years before *Veritatis Splendor*, *The Natural Law According to Aquinas and Suárez* admirably explains why "only God can answer the question about what is good, because he is the Good itself."[119] And in this way, Walter R. Farrell, O.P., shows himself to be a true Catholic theologian and a faithful member of the Thomist Tradition.

*~ Cajetan Cuddy, O.P.*
*Couvent Saint-Albert-le-Grand*
*Fribourg, Switzerland*
*Ash Wednesday 2019*

118. Farrell, *Natural Law According to Aquinas and Suárez*, p. xlv.
119. *Veritatis Splendor*, §9.

* * *

# Author's Introduction

The subject of the Natural Moral Law is attracting a great deal of attention today in the fields of Catholic philosophy and theology as well as in the natural sciences, such as anthropology. This statement is borne out by a glance at any of the excellent European philosophical and theological reviews of today, for example *Ephemerides Theologicae Lovanienses* (April 1929) and *Revue des Sciences Philosophiques et Theologiques* (July 1929). As for the natural sciences, the author has had the opportunity of hearing discussions on this subject by eminent scientists in America and of noting the seriousness of the question from their point of view.

Reasons for this interest are not hard to assign. On the part of Catholic philosophy and theology, the return to the scientific thoroughness of the early Schoolmen which followed naturally on the movement back to Scholasticism, particularly to the doctrine of St. Thomas, has undoubtedly had a great part to play. The advance in scientific knowledge and investigation, giving concrete opportunities of applying and testing existing explanations of the Natural Moral Law, has also been a strong factor in the rejection of much that was little more than unwarranted guesswork and in the earnest effort to put the whole question on a solid basis.

Another element that has added, perhaps unconsciously, to the interest of this question is the phenomenon of peoples abandoning Christianity, and sometimes even turning to rank atheism, yet maintaining a definite moral code, frequently in open violation of all laws of logic. This has prompted the question as to whether this morality was the result of an unconscious Christian heritage or whether it flowed from nature itself, from a source that no amount of rhetoric could influence.

Whatever the reason for it, the interest is beyond doubt a healthy one and very sadly necessary; for the question of the Natural Moral Law is in urgent need of solution. Ignorance of the nature of this law has gone to incredible lengths outside the Church; and this not only among the people of ordinary education, but among the most learned. It is only such ignorance that allows Dr. Robert Andrews Millikan, winner of a Nobel prize and certainly one of the greatest scientific minds in America today, to hail as marvelous discoveries truths that have been commonplace in the Church from the beginning of the Christian era. As he is quoted in *The Literary Digest* for October 12, 1929, he makes such statements as these: "The ancient world...believed that God, or Nature, or the Universe, whichever term you prefer, was a being of caprice and whim. Today, however, we think of a God who rules through law, or a Nature capable of being depended on, or a Universe of consistency, or orderliness, and of the beauty that goes with order. This idea has made modern science, and it is unquestionably the foundation of modern civilization...it is not merely the material side of life that this idea has changed. It has also revolutionized the whole mode of thought of the race. It has changed the philosophical and religious conceptions of mankind," etc.

Among our own philosophers there is such lamentable confusion of theories and opinions that the outsider can well be pardoned his lack of courage to investigate the problem. Leaving aside for the moment the differences between the older theologians, even neglecting all minor questions and difficulties, and considering only the very essence of the Natural Moral Law, we find a modern author,[1] in the brief scope allowed to a philosophical textbook, obliged to quote these six opinions: (a) the Natural Moral Law is the Eternal Law; (b) it is the rational nature in itself; (c) it is a habit; (d) it is the intellect itself, the light of reason; (e) it is the dictate of reason showing the good to be done; (f) it is the act of judgment of the reason.

Nor is our task the mere selection of one of these six opinions; the author pauses just long enough, in enumerating these theories, effectively to refute each one. Evidently it is time that some definite, well-established ideas were proposed on this subject. Fortunately such ideas have been proposed recently and are still being proposed today.

It is not the purpose of this dissertation to add one more theory to the many now flourishing. The aim of this work is not to create, expose, or defend a new theory; it is rather to dig out the explanation of St. Thomas from the mass of commentaries and interpretations that are threatening to smother it, to set forth

1. Leonardus Lehu, O.P., *Philosophia Moralis et Socialis* (Paris: Lecoffre, 1914), vol. 1, p. 239.

the explanation of St. Thomas, as given by Thomas, and, as far as possible, in the words of the Angelic Doctor.

With this end in view, the principal sources used in this dissertation have been the works of St. Thomas himself. The method followed has been:

(1) To give as clear and thorough an explanation as possible of St. Thomas's doctrine on law in general and on the Eternal Law; as these two contain the principles of his teaching on the Natural Moral Law and an understanding of them is quite essential to a full grasp of the Natural Moral Law.

(2) To expose the theory of Suárez on law, the Eternal Law and the Natural Moral Law, criticizing the first two immediately, the third only at the end of the last chapter when the doctrine of St. Thomas has been fully explained. The purpose of examining the doctrine of Suárez was to further clarify that of St. Thomas and to emphasize the essential elements of the Thomistic teaching by contrast with Suárez's theory which is quite diametrically opposed to it.

(3) To expose St. Thomas's doctrine on the essence of the Natural Moral Law and on the problems more immediately connected with this key problem, not going contrary to the traditional Thomistic doctrine, but rather going farther, at times, in the same direction.

It is a well-known fact to students of St. Thomas that the Angelic Doctor had, in all its perfection, that scholastic characteristic of brief, comprehensive, exact, and very profound definition. This required a complete grasp of the subject as well as the truths immediately connected with it, along with an exact terminology whose meaning was known to the learned world. As a result of this, a comprehension of what is contained in these brief, simple-looking definitions can be had only on the same terms that were prerequisites of their formulation. This is the explanation, perhaps, of why a learned world that has lost not only the terminology but even many of the essential truths, condemns these profound syntheses as vague generalizations. What was once so clear to the great thinkers of Scholasticism has become almost unintelligible to the twentieth century.

Perhaps the best expression of the aim of this dissertation would be to say it hopes to bring out some of the intellectual treasures that St. Thomas put into his profound definitions and explanations of law, the Eternal Law, and the Natural Moral Law.

* * *

# Chapter I

## The Notion of Law

The etymological derivation of the word "law" is uncertain. The three most famous derivations of the word are those adopted by St. Thomas, St. Isidore, and St. Augustine who derive the word respectively from "*ligare*," "*legere*" and "*eligere*."[1] Thus St. Thomas, in his derivation, stresses the essential binding power of law; St. Isidore its permanency; and St. Augustine the prudence with which laws should be framed. Which of these derivations is correct is a question of little importance; certainly each of them expresses some quality which law enjoys, and so all are quite plausible.

Whatever its derivation, the term "law" has been used in widely different senses. In this dissertation we shall make a definite distinction between laws properly so-called and improperly so-called. Laws properly so-called we shall restrict to those laws which regulate the moral actions of men; all other so-called laws we shall consider as laws improperly so-called, such as physical laws, laws of art, etc., all of which will be outside our consideration.

Taken in this sense, the existence of law is evident from a glance at any modern government. The necessity of law is no less evident from our daily experience. What is not so evident is the *reason* for this existence of law, the *reason* for its necessity, the essential nature of law itself. At least the solution of these problems is not easy for the man outside the Church. For the Catholic these answers are logical, inevitable corollaries deduced from basic Catholic truths, from the teaching of the Church on the creation and the government of the world and on the nature of man.

From the Catholic principles—that the world was created and is governed by One, Personal, Supremely Intelligent God,[2] and that man is a rational animal,[3] i.e., possessing an immortal soul and enjoying reason and free will, yet defectible because he is a creature—we have, as simple deductions, all the essential notions connected with law. Let us consider the Catholic teaching for a moment.

We have held before our eyes as the creator of the world this One, Personal God, Supremely Intelligent.[4] What mode of action could be expected, or rather demanded, from such a Supreme Being as He sets about His work of creation and consequent government of the world? At the very least He would have a definite plan of this creation in His mind before beginning the work.[5] We would demand this much from an intelligent man.

1. *ST* I-II, q. 90, a. 1; St. Isidore, *Originum libri*, lib. II, c. 10; and St. Augustine, *Quaest. XX de Levitico*.
2. *ST* I, q. 4, aa. 1, 2, 3; I, q. 44, a. 1; I, q. 103, a. 1 and a. 3.
3. *SCG* II, c. 56–72; *ST* I, q. 75, *proemium*; I, q. 78, a. 1.
4. Cf. note 3.
5. *SCG* III, c. 1 and 2; *ST* I-II, q. 93, a. 1.

Granting this much, which cannot be denied, it follows that in the mind of God there was a very definite choice of means to attain the end that He had in view in creating; a choice of efficacious means, rules of guidance of His work to its end, a decision as to the manner in which He would direct the work to its end. We must see at once the marvelous scope of these means to attain the end of creation, for they must extend to every created thing. At the same time we see clearly how they must be adapted to the diversity of natures created by God, how each creature must be directed to the great end in a manner suitable to the nature given it by the Creator.

These conclusions from the nature of the Creator contain all the essential notions of the Eternal Law, the source of all law; and at the same time they contain the explanation of the existence of all laws among men, as will be apparent from the following pages of this chapter.

From the Catholic doctrine on man we have conclusions no less pertinent. The Church teaches that man is a creature of body and soul,[6] the king of creatures in this world because of his spiritual side, because of his great gifts of reason and free will. Yet, for all that, still a creature, capable of failure, defectible.[7] It is evident then that man, being a creature, a part of this work of creation which was intelligently planned for an end, also has some very definite part to play in creation, some definite end to attain. It is no less evident that, being by nature defectible, he needs guidance, helpful rules of conduct to assist him in reaching his end.

6. Concil. Toletanum, XV, 688, *Protestatio de Trinitate et Incarnatione*, *Denzinger* 295, p. 133.

7. *ST* I, q. 63, a. 1, *corp.*

This direction of man must first of all be a direction of reason, since man is a creature of reason, capable of knowing the end and of choosing the means to the end. Because he enjoys free will, man can use his freedom to follow this guidance of reason or he can abuse his liberty and refuse to follow—so the compelling force behind these guiding rules must be moral, not physical. In a word, man can be guided to the end for which he was created only by a moral law, a rule of reason given to reasonable creatures and carrying with it a moral obligation. God must have selected some reasonable, moral rules of conduct, applicable to all men—for human nature is everywhere the same—yet at the same time within the reach of every individual human being, known or at least capable of being known by every man. These rules of conduct we know as the Natural Moral Law.

A few more very obvious conclusions from these fundamental truths could be easily drawn, conclusions which would be no more than the short finishing strokes that would complete the miniature of law as contained in Catholic teaching. But the deductions we have already made are quite sufficient for our purpose in this dissertation, as they contain the essential notions of law as far as we shall treat of them.

It is to be noted that this guidance, these rules, have the one ultimate source and are all for the one ultimate purpose of helping man to attain the end for which he was created, of guiding him that he might not select means which would rather divert him from this end. Or, to put the same truth in other words, all true law is for the express purpose of protecting man's liberty, not of limiting or destroying it;[8] for liberty, in its

8. Dominicus M. Prümmer, O.P., *Manuale Theologiae Moralis Secundum Principia*

ultimate resolution means nothing more than a choice of means leading *to* an end.[9†]

This obvious inclusion of all the essential elements of law in fundamental truths perhaps explains the sporadic nature of the writings of the Fathers on this subject, none of whom wrote a complete and *ex professo* tract on laws. It was unnecessary and there were so many other questions which demanded immediate attention and explanation. It remained for the Scholastics (perhaps Alexander of Hales was the first) with their scientific treatment of all doctrine, to give the question exhaustive treatment.

## I. Explanation and Proof of Thomistic Definition

St. Thomas had breathed deeply of this scientific atmosphere; at the same time he had a full knowledge, a profound intimacy with the basic truths upon which law is founded. It was with such a background that he wrote his classical definition of law, which we have only to quote and explain to give a full exposition of Thomistic teaching on law. But before proceeding to this definition, let us note that we are speaking of law in a still more restricted sense than moral law in general. Law, strictly taken, can be spoken of in three ways: as it is in him who makes the law, the legislator, as in the one regulating; as it is in him for whom the

*S. Thomae Aquinatis*, vol. 1 (Freiburg im Breisgau: Herder, 1928), vol. I, p. 101, no. 144.

9. *ST* I, q. 62, a. 8, ad. 3.

† **Editor's Note:** For a more recent account of the liberating character of all true law, see part three ("Freedom and Natural Law") of Servais Pinckaers, O.P., *The Sources of Christian Ethics,* trans. Sr. Mary Thomas Noble, O.P. (Washington, DC: The Catholic University of America Press, 1995), pp. 325–456.

law is made, the subject, as in the one regulated; finally as it is contained in some permanent external medium, for example in a book or code of laws.[10] In this definition, St. Thomas is speaking of law in the first sense, as it is in the legislator as in the one regulating. In this sense law is "a certain ordination of reason for the common good, made by him who has care of the community and promulgated."[11]

**1. "A certain ordination of reason."** The word "ordination" shows us that St. Thomas is speaking of the practical intellect as opposed to the speculative intellect; ordination is the work of prudence, which is an act of the practical intellect.[12] That is, law has to do with things to be done rather than with things merely to be known.[13] It is the term of this act of the practical intellect, not the act itself, the proposition of the practical intellect corresponding to the proposition of the speculative intellect, that St. Thomas means by this first phrase of his definition.[14]

But not every proposition of the practical intellect is a law. This would include counsels and particular precepts, i.e., precepts given to individuals by any superior. This proposition of the practical intellect is a precept, i.e., the "*imperium*" of the intellect commanding that which the will has chosen; an act essentially of the intellect, since it is ordinative and regulative, but implying a previous act of the will from which it has its motive power.[15] Since precept deals only with the means to the end, not the end itself, it

10. *ST* I-II, q. 90, a. 1 ad 1; Billuart, *Tract. de Legibus,* Diss. I, a.1.
11. *ST* I-II, q. 90, a. 4.
12. *ST* II-II, q. 47, a. 8; ibid., a. 2.
13. *ST* I-II, q. 90, a. 1 ad 2; ibid., q. 93, a. 1, *corp.*
14. *ST* I, q. 79, a. 11.
15. *ST* I-II, q. 17, a. 1, *corp.* and ad 1; *ST* II-II, q. 47, a. 8, *corp.* and ad 3.

is apparent that St. Thomas limits law to the ordination of means to an end—"*ad bonum commune.*"[16]

This point, namely of precept being essentially an act of reason, must be particularly stressed for it is the characteristic which distinguishes the teaching of St. Thomas on law from the voluntarism of Suárez. We shall treat of this more fully in our third chapter, in criticizing the doctrine of Suárez; for the present it will be sufficient to note that St. Thomas put this doctrine in his usual brief and profound way when he said that "law... is a general precept."[17] With a slight notion of what St. Thomas meant by precept, this short phrase also gives an indication of another characteristic of the Thomistic doctrine on law, which will also be brought out more clearly as this dissertation proceeds; that is, that the primary purpose of law is that it regulate human actions. It is above all a rule or norm of action since it is a precept and so ordains to action[18]; the idea obligation, though of course essential, is not the element particularly stressed in the thought of St. Thomas; it is rather a corollary from the nature of precept.

To be law this dictate of practical reason must be efficacious, at least in causing an obligation on the part of the subject, which is again only saying that it must be a true precept.[19] It must be firm and perpetual in the sense that it does not cease with the death of the legislator, nor is it made only for present but also for future subjects. The reason for this is that the community, for

16. *ST* II-II, q. 47, a. 8; ibid., q. 50; *ST* I-II, q. 90, a. 4.

17. "Lex...est enim preceptum commune" (I-II, q. 98, a. 6 ad 2).

18. *ST* I-II, q. 17, a. 1.

19. *Quodlib.*, V, q. 10, a. 1; cf. Dom Odon Lottin, O.S.B., "La Définition Classique de la Loi," *Revue Néo-Scolastique de Philosophie*, Vol. 27, No. 7 (1925): pp. 243–73 (p. 272).

which the law is made, is considered to be firm and perpetual.[20] St. Thomas himself indicates this when he says: "the community of the state is composed of many persons; and its good is procured by many actions; nor is it established to endure for only a short time, but to last for all time by the citizens succeeding one another, as Augustine says."[21]

The statement that law is an ordination of reason is readily proved by St. Thomas.[22] The distinguishing mark between the acts of man and the brutes is that man's actions are always ordained to an end by man himself; they proceed from the will, under the attracting influence of the end, but are human acts, i.e., distinctively from man, only insofar as they are directed, ordained to this end by reason. In other words, human acts are essentially deliberate. It is the reason which does that which the brutes cannot do—see the end, judge the means to that end and ordain and direct these means to the end in view; it is the reason that makes human acts really such. In a word, it is the reason which is the first principle in human acts, as human acts. This ordering of actions to an end is precisely the chief work of law; we have then a perfect parallel between the work of reason and of law so that it follows that law is essentially a thing of reason.[23]

This argument is advanced in a metaphysical way by St. Thomas on the basis of the principle that what is first in any

20. Charles-René Billuart, O.P., *Summa Sancti Thomae Hodiernis Academiarum Moribus Accommodata*, Vol. 4, *Tractatus de Legibus*, Diss. I, a. 1.

21. "Constituitur enim communitas civitatis ex multis personis; et eius bonum per multiplices actiones procuratur; nec ad hoc solum instituitur quod aliquo modico tempore duret, sed quod omni tempore perseveret per civium successionem, ut Augustinus dicit, in XXII de Civ. Dei" (*ST* I-II, q. 96, a. 1).

22. *ST* I-II, q. 90, a. 1.

23. Ibid.

order or genus is the rule or measure of that order.[24] Applying this principle to actions, we see that the end is the first principle of every action; without the end no action would be placed and consequently, in accordance with this principle, all actions are judged by the end, according as they do or do not lead to the attainment of the end.[25] Bringing this principle down still further to the actions of man, we see that for a specific determination of this rule or measure of human actions, we must determine definitely what is the end of human actions.[†]

Since the end of every nature is its ultimate perfection, or in other words the perfection of its form, and the form of human nature is the rational soul, the natural end of man will be the perfection of his rational nature: "the good of everything consists in the fact that its operation is suited to its form. Now the distinctive form of man is that which makes him a rational animal. Hence man's action must be good precisely because it harmonizes with right reason."[26] All the actions of man will be judged good or bad according as they lead to this end or detract from its attainment. But this end, precisely as it is the rule or norm of human actions, is in reason (*finis in intentione*), it is the ideal of his nature for which he is striving. His acts are good or bad, then, according

24. Ibid.

25. Ibid.

† **Editor's Note:** For a helpful consideration of the radical primacy of the end within the context of human action, see Steven A. Long, "Speculative Foundations of Moral Theology and the Causality of Grace," *Studies in Christian Ethics*, Vol. 23, No. 4 (2010): pp. 397–414.

26. "Bonum cuiuslibet rei est in hoc quod sua operatio sit conveniens suae formae. Propria autem forma hominis est secundum quam est animal rationale. Unde oportet quod operatio hominis sit bona ex hoc, quod est secundum rationem rectam" (*II Ethicorum*, lect. 2, no. 257). Cf. *ST* I-II, q. 18, a. 5; ibid., q. 100, a. 1.

as they are in accordance with this right reason or opposed to it, according as they are reasonable or unreasonable. Reason, as containing the end of human actions (*finis in intentione*), is thus the principle of human acts; and, like the first in any order, it is the norm of that order, the rule of human actions. Since this is precisely the work of law, it follows that law is a thing of reason.

This argument brings out very strongly the opposition of St. Thomas to those who maintain that law is essentially the work of the will. It is true that some movement of the will is necessary, namely election, as we shall show more exhaustively later on; and, at least as regards positive laws, also a movement of application. But no such movement of regulation or measuring, such as pertains to the essence of law, is attributed by St. Thomas to the will.[27] Indeed the will is incapable of such a movement for it is a *blind* faculty; so for an act of the will to become a law it would be necessary for the will to have both the movement and regulation of the intellect, while the intellect needs only the movement of application from the will.[28] St. Thomas himself tells us that the will unregulated by the intellect is rather wickedness than law.[29] It is the opinion of some of the other authors, certainly Sylvius and perhaps Billuart, that even this movement of the will is not required for the efficacy of Eternal Law.[30] But we will touch on this question in the following chapter.

St. Thomas proposes another argument to prove his position; an argument which shows more clearly the part played by the will

27. *ST* I-II, q. 17, a. 1, *corp.* and ad 1; Billuart, *Tractatus de Legibus*, Diss. I, a.1.
28. Cajetan in I II, q. 90, a. 1 ad 3.
29. *ST* I-II, q. 90, a. 1 ad 3.
30. Billuart, *Tractatus de Legibus*, Diss. I, a.1; Sylvius in I-II, q. 90, a. 1, concl. III.

in law, as it is drawn from his treatment of the acts imperated by the will.[31]

In the first article he asks whether "*imperium*" or command is an act of the reason or of the will. His answer is that essentially this "command" is an act of the reason because it ordains him, to whom the command is given, to action; and this ordination is by way of intimation or denunciation, which is essentially an act of the reason. There is however an act of the will presupposed, by whose power the reason moves to the exercise of the act. Applying this teaching to law, we find that to give precepts and to prohibit, in other words to command, is the work of law; as has already been proved, to command is the work of the reason, so that law must pertain essentially to reason, though it presupposes a movement of the will by the power of which the reason moves through the "*imperium*" to action.[32]

A glance at St. Thomas's *ex professo* treatment of "*imperium*" leaves no doubt as to the part he assigns to the will in this act. It is self-evident that ordination, taken precisely as such, i.e., the orderly arrangement of things in view of an end to be obtained, is the work of intelligence. Consequently it is reserved to reason; it is impossible of accomplishment by a blind faculty such as the will. The question as to the possibility of this act being from the will arises when we add to this ordination the idea of command, the idea of movement ordered, as St. Thomas puts it, "*intimando vel denuntiando*," i.e., by effective command.

The will is unquestionably the first principle of all free movement in man; but St. Thomas leaves no room for equivocation

31. *ST* I-II, q. 17, a. 1.

32. *ST* I-II, q. 90, a. 1 *sed contra*; ibid., q. 17, a. 1.

when he develops his thought by saying: "Now the reason can intimate or declare [*intimare vel denuntiare*] something in two ways. First, absolutely: and this intimation is expressed by a verb in the indicative mood, as when one person says to another: 'This is what you should do.' Sometimes, however, the reason intimates something to a man by moving him thereto; and this intimation is expressed by a verb in the imperative mood; as when it is said to someone: 'Do this.'"[33] That is, not only the ordination contained in "*imperium*," but also the movement of effective command is essentially the work of the reason. The difficulty of the will is solved by St. Thomas in the same way that he solves the difficulty of the reasonableness of the election of the will; i.e., just as the election participates in the preceding judgment of the reason and is thus reasonable, so "*imperium*" of the reason participates in the preceding election of the will and in this way has the power to move. We shall treat this question more exhaustively in our third chapter; here it is only necessary to insist on the true thought of St. Thomas.

**2. "To the common good."**[†] This is the second part of St. Thomas's definition of law. It refers to the common good of the community, which good is defined by St. Thomas as the happiness

33. "Sed ratio potest aliquid intimare vel denuntiare dupliciter. Uno modo, absolute, quae quidem intimatio exprimitur per verbum indicativi modi; sicut si aliquis alicui dicat, hoc est tibi faciendum. Aliquando autem ratio intimat aliquid alicui, movendo ipsum ad hoc, et talis intimatio exprimitur per verbum imperativi modi; puta cum alicui dicitur, fac hoc" (*ST* I-II, q. 17, a. 1). See also ad 1.

† **Editor's Note:** The common good remained a subject of interest for Farrell. He later addressed this topic in relation to various political and social questions in his ten-part essay (co-authored with Mortimer J. Adler) titled "The Theory of Democracy" that was published in *The Thomist* from 1941 to 1944.

34. *ST* I-II, q. 90, a. 2.

of that community.[34] This is only another way of saying that the common good of the community consists in the attainment of its final end, i.e., in the perfection of the form of that community, since the good of every nature is in the perfection of its form,[35] and a society is a moral being or nature.

The final end of man is his happiness; a supernatural happiness, it is true, but not all communities have to deal with leading man to his supernatural end directly.[†] Nevertheless they have at least to do with the attainment of his secondary ends of natural or temporal happiness, which are a means to the supernatural final end.[36] As law is primarily an ordination or regulation of human acts to an end, it follows that it should deal above all with the direction of these acts to the supreme or final end. That this is the purpose of law is proved from the common consent of men who immediately protest the enforcement of a law that is against the common good. It can also be shown by induction, by a momentary consideration of different laws, bearing in mind the fact that the common good can be obtained either directly or indirectly, i.e., by benefiting the community immediately or mediately by benefiting certain individuals.[37]

St. Thomas proves that the common good is the end of law, the reason for its existences. Law pertains to that which is the principle of human acts—reason—from the fact that it is a rule and measure of these acts, as we have already shown. Just as reason is the principle of human acts, so also in the practical

35. *II Ethic.* lect. 2; cf. *ST* I-II, q. 18, a. 5; ibid., q. 1, a. 5.

† **Editor's Note:** See Steven A. Long, "Understanding the Common Good," *Nova et Vetera*, Vol. 16, No. 4 (2018): pp. 1135–52.

36. Gonet, *Manuale Thomistarum*, Tract. VI, c. 1 (p. 245).

37. Billuart, *Tract. de Legibus*, Diss. I, a. 1.

reason itself there is something which is the principle with respect to everything else; hence it is to this principle of principles that law must principally and chiefly pertain. This principle of principles, the very first principle in things to be done, with which the practical reason deals, is the final end of man, happiness or beatitude. Further, since every part is ordained to the whole, as the imperfect to the perfect, and since every man is a part of a perfect community, it is necessary that law properly deal with the order to the common happiness.[38]

It is to be noted that the common good mentioned here is that of a perfect community,[39] which may be defined as a society, *sui iuris*, having in itself its own sufficient means to attain its proper end and independent, in its own order, of every other society.[40] The reason for this restriction of law to a perfect society is pointed out by St. Thomas himself when he says that after all man is a part of society (being by nature social) and it would be unreasonable to invert the welfare of the whole to that of the part, just as it would be unreasonable to order the perfect to the imperfect. It is of a perfect community that man constitutes a part.[41]

**3. "By him who has care of the community."** In this third part of his definition, St. Thomas points out the author of law. No private person has the right or power to legislate for the whole community; there is no reason why this individual's command should be imposed on the community rather than the command of any other member of the community. Only the community

38. *ST* I-II, q. 90, a. 2.

39. *ST* I-II, q. 90, a. 3 ad 3.

40. Prümmer, *Manuale Theologiae Moralis*, vol. 1, p. 100, no. 143.

41. *ST* I-II, q. 90, a. 2.

itself, its vicar or he who has care of it, has the right and power to legislate. Law first and principally has to do with the ordination to the common good or to the final end; and it is the sole right of him to whom the end is proper to ordain the means to that end.[42] Here again St. Thomas is insisting on the rationality of law. It is not something extrinsic imposed by the will of the superior; it is the regulation of actions to an end and so is nothing more than the expression of the reason of the community for which the law is made.

Cajetan points out here that St. Thomas uses two expressions, namely, "the vicar of the community" and "he who has care of the community." St. Thomas does not use these as synonymous terms; rather in the use of the former he is speaking in a restricted sense of human legislators, and in the use of the latter he is speaking universally so that the term is universally true, even being applicable to the supreme Legislator, God.[43]

**4. "Promulgated."** This fourth and last part of St. Thomas's definition of law is inserted in the definition, says Billuart,[44] just as "obscurity" is included in the definition of faith; that is, it does not pertain to the essence of law but is a necessary condition, a *proprium*.[45] This is easily seen because law would hardly oblige men if they did not know the law; which is precisely the purpose of promulgation—to make the law known. That it does not pertain to the essence of law is equally evident from our consideration of law as a rule or measure; promulgation is rather the

42. *ST* I-II, q. 90, a. 3.
43. Cajetan, in I-II, q. 90, a. 3.
44. Billuart, *Tract. de Legibus*, Diss. I, a. 3 ad 2.
45. *ST* I-II, q. 90, a. 4.
46. *ST* I-II, q. 90, a. 4.

application of this rule or measure than a constitution of it.[46]

Philosophically this same truth can be proved by a consideration of the nature of essences.[47] It is only required that the essence have the power or aptitude required of the particular nature which it constitutes. Law would have this essential aptitude to regulate and measure human acts before its promulgation or without it; promulgation merely completes the law "*in actu secundo*," or in other words, it brings it down to actual application, makes it actually oblige here and now. The discussion as to whether promulgation pertains to the essence of law is not of any great value as far as the obligation of the law is concerned. All agree that no man is bound by a law until it has been promulgated. But it may be of some utility in our discussion of the nature of the Eternal Law and the Natural Moral Law.

## II. Distinction from Counsel and Precept

From this discussion of the definition of law, we see how law differs from a counsel. The latter carries with it no notion of strict obligation, such as is always to be found in law, and counsel can be given by a private person.[48] Thus too we see that law differs from a simple precept (one given to a particular person or persons) in three ways: law is given for the community, precept for particular persons; law is perpetual in the sense already explained, simple precept is temporal; law can be framed only by him who has care of a perfect

47. Billuart, *Tract. de Legibus*, Diss. I, a. 3, Dico 2, prob. 2.

48. *ST* I-II, q. 92, a. 2 ad 2.

49. Jean-Baptiste Gonet, O.P., *Manuale Thomistarum, seu Totius Theologiae Brevis Cursus in Gratiam et Commodum Studentium Editus* (Venice: 1745), Tract. VI, c. 1, p. 245.

community, precept can be given by any legitimate superior.[49]

The difference between law and a common or universal precept (given to the whole community) is not so clear. St. Thomas himself says: "law...is a general precept,"[50] thus plainly identifying law and common precept. But today the term precept does not seem to have the same general meaning attached to it by St. Thomas. There is a great variety of opinion on this question, which after all is not of such great importance. In the sense in which we use the word, this one distinctive mark seems to cling even to the common precept, namely that it is temporal in the sense that it ceases to oblige with the death of the superior; while law is negatively perpetual.[51] This question will come up again in our discussion of the precepts of the Natural Moral Law, but as St. Thomas clearly defines his terms in speaking of these precepts, we will have no difficulty in this matter.

## III. Acts and Effects of Law

St. Thomas assigns four "acts" to law[52]; but of course these are not acts properly so-called, since law is neither a potency nor a habit and so cannot have an act.[53] The sense meant by St. Thomas is that these things pertain to the integrity of law. They are to be found in all laws; not necessarily at one and the same time, but in the sense that no laws exist that do not contain at least one or the other of these acts. They are: to command, to prohibit, to permit,

50. "Lex...est enim preceptum commune" (*ST* I-II, q. 98, a. 6 ad 2).

51. Gonet, *Manuale Thomistarum*, Tract. VI, c. 1 (p. 245).

52. *ST* I-II, q. 92, a. 2.

53. Billuart, *Tract. de Legibus*, Diss. I, a. 5, Dico 2, nota.

54. *ST* I-II, q. 92, a. 2.

and to punish.[54]

We see at once that these four acts correspond to the different human acts. Thus good acts are commanded, bad acts are prohibited and punished, indifferent acts are permitted. It is to be noticed that "to oblige" is not mentioned among these acts of law; obligation is included in all four acts. Even permission carries with it the idea of obligation insofar as it obliges others not to interfere with the carrying out of the permission.[55] Indeed the notion of obligation is included in the very notion of precept and consequently of law, as St. Thomas tells us: "precept conveys the notion of something due."[56]

The effect of law is to make men good, since its end is to ordain men to their final end.[57] But we must note with St. Thomas, that not all laws make men good, "simply speaking" that is, in the sense that the moral virtues make men good: every law makes men good, at least in the sense that it makes them fulfill one of their duties, that of obedience as citizens.[58]

## IV. Division of Law

The division of law, which in its various ramifications need not concern us, can be summed up for our purposes as follows[59]:

55. Billuart, *Tract. de Legibus*, Diss. I, a. 5, Dico 2, Inst.
56. "Preceptum importat rationem debiti" (*Quodlib.*, V, q. 10, a. 1).
57. *ST* I-II, q. 92, a. 1.
58. Ibid., *corp.*, *sed contra*, ad 3 and ad 4; Billuart, *Tract. de Legibus*, Diss. I, a. 5, Dico 1, nota.
59. Prümmer, *Manuale Theologiae Moralis*, vol. 1, pp. 101–2, no. 146.

1. Divine Law—whose immediate author is God:
    (a) Eternal Law—the reason of divine wisdom according as it is directive of all creatures to their final end.
    (b) Natural Moral Law—the participation of the Eternal Law in rational creature.
    (c) Divine Positive Law—contained in the Old and New Testament; promulgated by a special divine revelation.
2. Human Law—law framed by human authority:
    (a) Ecclesiastical—framed by ecclesiastical authority.
    (b) Civil—framed by civil authority.

* * *

# Chapter II

## The Eternal Law

A thorough grasp of the Eternal Law is essential for a profound understanding of the Natural Moral Law. The same is true, indeed, of all laws, since the Eternal Law is the source from which all are derived[1]; but it is particularly true of the Natural Moral Law, not only because of its more immediate derivation from, but also because of its intimate connection with the Eternal Law.

From the point of view of derivation, the Natural Moral Law is derived from the Eternal through the medium of natural reason; while human laws are derived through the mediums of human reason and human authority.[2] But over and above this derivation, the connection between the Eternal Law and the Natural Moral Law is so intimate that St. Thomas could give a comprehensive definition of the latter by simply stating that it was a "participation of the Eternal Law in a rational creature"[3]; and this definition has been repeated as adequate by philosophers and theologians since the time of St. Thomas.

## I. Connection with the Natural Law

The connection of these two laws is often stated more strongly. For example the Natural Moral Law is called a "promulgation" of the Eternal Law[4]; or it is said that the ordination of all things, in the mind of God, pertaining to rational nature is the Eternal Law, the impression of this ordination on the mind of man is the Natural Moral Law[5]; or again that the Eternal Law, passively taken, coincides with the Natural Moral Law.[6] There is then more than sufficient reason for including a thorough treatment of the Eternal Law in a dissertation dealing with the Natural Moral Law.

## II. Existence of the Eternal Law

The existence of such an Eternal Law is proved by St. Thomas from his doctrine on providence, on the divine intellect and his general tract on law. The world was created by God,[7] an intelligent agent; consequently, it was created for a definite end. To attain that end it is governed, directed by God.[8] The order of the world to its end is no less a created thing than the material substance of the world itself; consequently, since this order is the result of an intelligent creation, it postulates a pre-existing plan

1. *ST* I-II, q. 93, a. 3.
2. Gonet, *Manuale Thomistarum*, Tract. VI, *De Legibus*, c. II, p. 248.
3. *ST* I-II, q. 91, a. 2.
4. Joseph Gredt, O.S.B., *Elementa Philosophiae Aristotelico-Thomisticae*, 4th ed. (Freiburg im Breisgau: Herder, 1926), Vol. II, p. 287.
5. Prümmer, *Manuale Theologiae Moralis*, Vol. I, p. 105, no. 151.
6. Christoph Willems, *Philosophia Moralis* (Trier, 1908), Vol. III, p. 107.
7. *ST* I, q. 44, a. 1.
8. *ST* I, q. 103; *SCG* III, c. 64.

in the mind of God, i.e., providence.[9] Providence, or the order of things to their end existing in the mind of God, being established, the existence of the Eternal Law is evident from a mere application of the general principles of law laid down by St. Thomas and explained in our first chapter.

According to these principles, law is nothing more than the dictate of practical reason in the governor of a perfect community; the "*ratio gubernationis*" or "*ratio providentiae*," as St. Thomas expresses it in other passages,[10] has the essential elements of law.[11] The mind of St. Thomas is evident: he is considering providence as one phase of the government of the world, the actual execution of this providence as the other phase, as he has already said explicitly in the *Prima Pars*: "Two things pertain to the care of providence—namely, the 'reason of order,' which is called providence and disposition; and the execution of order, which is termed government. Of these, the first is eternal, and the second is temporal."[12] The "*ratio*" or foundation of these two aspects, a dictate of the divine practical intellect, is the Eternal Law. St. Thomas is drawing an almost perfect corollary from his general treatment of law, as is evident from the article treating of the existence of the Eternal Law.[13]

This law governing the universe is strictly a law and is eternal. Of the eternity there can be no question; the law exists in the

9. *ST* I, q. 22, a. 1.

10. *ST* I-II, q. 93, a. 5, ad 3; *SCG* III, c. 115, c. 121, etc.; *De Veritate*, q. 5, a. 1, ad 6.

11. *ST* I-II, q. 91, a. 1, *corp.* and ad 1.

12. "Ad curam duo pertinent, scilicet ratio ordinis, quae dicitur providentia et dispositio; et executio ordinis, quae dicitur gubernatio. Quorum primum est aeternum, secundum temporale" (*ST* I, q. 22, a. 1, ad 2).

13. *ST* I-II, q. 91, a. 1.

mind of God, Who conceives nothing in time but has an eternal concept.[14] The claim that this is a law in strict sense will be abundantly evident when we treat of the essence of this law. One obvious difficulty may suggest itself here, namely that since the law is eternal, it could not possibly be promulgated. We have shown in Chapter One that promulgation does not pertain to the essence of law, but rather to the application of law, or law "*in actu secundo*."

Even though the Eternal Law could not be promulgated from eternity, it would still have the essential notes of law from eternity. But there was certainly one element of promulgation present from eternity. Not, of course, on the part of the creature knowing the law, as the creature exists only in time,[15] but on the part of God. St. Thomas indicates this when he says that God ordered the government of things foreknown by him[16]; this short phrase is a very concise summary of a very profound doctrine. After the decree of the divine will in which God knows all actual things, these things were present to the divine mind as they are in themselves, not through any mental species, and for this reason the knowledge of God is said to be intuitive.

The eternity of God includes and far surpasses the whole extent of time. Thus the divine "*intuitus*" sees all things as they are present to the divine mind, as they are actually in themselves.[17] From the part of God, promulgation of this Eternal Law is quite perfect, as the creatures to whom the law is given are actually present to God; the defect comes from the part of the creatures,

14. Ibid., and *ST* I, q. 14, a. 4.
15. *ST* I-II, q. 91, a. 1, ad 2.
16. *ST* I-II, q. 91, a. 1, ad 1.
17. *ST* I, q. 14, a. 13, *corp.* and ad 3.

which do not know the law until they exist in time. As Billuart points out, the promulgation demanded of a law is not necessarily such as would make the law known to every subject actually existing but a promulgation by which the law can be known by a subject when he does actually exist. Thus human laws are promulgated not only for the present but also for the future citizens; in the same way, if man existed from eternity he would know the Eternal Law from eternity.[18]

## III. Essence of the Eternal Law

Coming down to a more profound examination of the exact nature of this law, we find St. Thomas has defined it as: "the eternal law is nothing else than the type of Divine Wisdom, as directing all actions and movements."[19] To understand all that is contained in this definition, it is highly important to note that St. Thomas expressly wished to retain, in explaining the Eternal Law, all the essential elements of law which he brought out in Question 90 of this tract on law and which we have explained in our first chapter. So we read: "the type in him who governs the acts of his subjects, bears the character of a law, provided the other conditions be present which we have mentioned above [*ST* I-II, q. 90]."[20]

Thus the Eternal Law will be the product of the divine practical intellect; moreover a precept of that practical intellect and

18. Billuart, *Tract. De Legibus*, Diss. II, a. 1.

19. "Lex aeterna nihil aliud est quam ratio divinae sapientiae, secundum quod est directiva omnium actuum et motionum" (*ST* I-II, q. 93, a. 1).

20. "Ratio gubernantis actus subditorum, rationem legis obtinet, servatis aliis quae supra esse diximus de legis ratione" (Ibid).

directive to the common good. All this is clearly brought out in the definition we have given: "*ratio divinae sapientiae*" ["type of the Divine Wisdom" (*ST* I-II, q. 93, a. 1)] indicates that the law is essentially of the intellect; inasmuch as it is described as "*directive omnium actuum*" ["directing all actions"], etc. it is clearly of the practical intellect as it deals with things to be done[21]; and it is a precept for it directs or ordains to an end[22]; that it is not only for the common good, but for the supreme common good or ultimate end, is also evident from the fact that it is a precept of the divine wisdom and the divine wisdom necessarily directs all its actions to the divine good, or final end of every created thing.[23]

The one fault that might be found with this definition is its inclusion of all things, not merely of rational creatures. Yet rational creatures are alone capable of receiving law, i.e., strictly taken as moral law. This is not an oversight on the part of St. Thomas, as is clear from the rest of the question; and we shall show that St. Thomas expressly held that only rational creatures were capable of receiving laws strictly so-called. But we will leave this discussion until we treat of the scope of the Eternal Law.

It will suffice for the present to get definite ideas of the essential notions contained in the Thomistic concept of Eternal Law. We have seen that St. Thomas considers the Eternal Law as an eternal precept of the divine practical intellect ordaining all things to the common or divine good and promulgated, incompletely, in eternity.

21. *ST* I, q. 79, a. 11.

22. *ST* II-II, q. 47, a. 8; *ST* I-II, q.17, a. 1.

23. *ST* I, q. 19, a. 2.

Before delving further into this question, we must note carefully the caution St. Thomas himself gives us in the *Summa Contra Gentiles*: "Now, the preceding statements are not to be understood in the sense that there is a difference between divine goodness, divine essence, and divine knowledge as it contains the arrangement of things; rather, there is a different way of considering each one."[24] In God all things are one except the subsistent relations; these distinctions we are making are rather from the part of our manner of consideration than from the part of God, but they are necessary for even our feeble understanding of divine things.

## IV. Distinction from Divine Ideas and Providence; Further Determination of Essence

We are now in a position to obtain a clearer and more profound knowledge of the Eternal Law by comparing it with the divine ideas and with providence. This comparison will show us the exact place of the Eternal Law in the divine mind.

The Eternal Law differs from the divine ideas in several ways easily perceived. Divine ideas are concerned solely with the ideal order, the merely possible, while the Eternal Law deals with things in the actual order, things definitely predetermined to exist. Consequently the divine ideas treat of things as possible of creation; the Eternal Law deals with things to be governed. Finally the divine ideas have a certain distinction and plurality inasmuch as they have reference to the distinct natures proper to singular

24. "Non autem sic praemissa intelligenda sunt quasi aliud sit divina bonitas, aliud divina essentia, et aliud eius scientia rerum dispositionem continens: sed quia secundum haec alia et alia est eius consideration" (*SCG* III, c. 80).

things; the Eternal Law, ordering all things to a common end, has an essential note of unity. These differences or their equivalents are noted by practically all the authors.[†]

The distinction between providence and the Eternal Law is not so easily seen. St. Thomas's definition of providence as "the type [*ratio*] of the order of things towards their end...pre-exist[ing] in the divine mind" [25††] may seem to come very close to his definition of the Eternal Law as "the type [*ratio*] of Divine Wisdom, as directing all actions and movements."[26] To add to this difficulty, Cajetan says briefly that divine providence, inasmuch as it is the measure and obligatory rule of all things, has the "*ratio legis*" ["character of law"].[27]

---

† **Editor's Note:** For a recent philosophical study of the divine ideas in Aquinas, see Gregory T. Doolan, *Aquinas on the Divine Ideas as Exemplar Causes* (Washington, DC: The Catholic University of America Press, 2014). See also: Vivian Boland, O.P., *Ideas in God According to Saint Thomas Aquinas* (Leiden: Brill, 1996); Serge-Thomas Bonino, O.P., *Thomas d'Aquin: De la Vérité ou La science en Dieu* (Paris/Fribourg: Éditions Universitaires de Fribourg Éditions du Cerf, 1996); Vincent P. Branick, "The Unity of the Divine Ideas," *The New Scholasticism*, Vol. 42, No. 2 (1968): pp. 171–201; David L. Greenstock, T.O.P., "Exemplar Causality and the Supernatural Order," *The Thomist*, Vol. 16, No. 1 (1953): pp. 1–13; Timothy Sparks, O.P., *De Divisione Causae Exemplaris apud S. Thomam* (River Forest, IL: Dominican House of Studies, 1936); Rudi A. te Velde, *Participation and Substantiality in Thomas Aquinas* (Leiden: Brill, 1995); John F. Wippel, *Thomas Aquinas on the Divine Ideas* (Toronto: Pontifical Institute of Mediaeval Studies, 1993).

25. "Ratio ordinis rerum in finem in mente divina praeexistat" (*ST* I, q. 22, a. 1).

†† **Editor's Note:** Farrell presents a slightly different Latin quotation from Aquinas in the original edition ("*ratio ordinis rerum in finem in mente divina existens*"). In this footnote, I have provided the actual Latin words found in Aquinas's text (taken from the 1953 Piana edition of the *Summa Theologiae*). However, the English translation provided above attempts to reflect the point Farrell originally wished to highlight.

26. "Ratio divinae sapientiae, secundum quod est directiva omnium actuum et motionum" (*ST* I-II, q. 93, a. 1).

27. Cajetan, in I-II, q. 91, a. 1.

This difficulty has been rather increased than lessened by the differences, very marked differences, pointed out by many of the authors.[28] Thus three differences are noted: (a) the Eternal Law has obligatory power, providence has not; (b) the Eternal Law deals with the common good of the universe, providence with the particular good of singular things; (c) the Eternal Law is like a principle, providence like the conclusion from this principle.

If we take the first two of these three differences in the obvious meaning of the words, they are quite opposed to the Thomistic teaching on providence. St. Thomas certainly taught that providence has obligatory power. Thus in his tract on providence, he reduces it to prudence and says providence "is the chief part of prudence,"[29] which is precept or command.[30] Further on in this same tract we find the following: "Providence, as also prudence, is the plan existing in the intellect directing the ordering of some things towards an end."[31]

This doctrine is confirmed by the interpretation of the Salamanticenses: "Providence...is placed in the act of the intellect, in which prudence consists: in precept and command.... If, however, providence was not preceptive [*praeceptiva*], and yet were to consist in a precept, St. Thomas would not have provided sufficient reason for what he had said: providence exists in the intellect, and thus is essentially an act of the intellect presupposing the act of willing an end...Providence not only presupposes

28. E.g., Billuart, *Tract. de Legibus*, Diss. II, a. 1.

29. "Est enim principalis pars prudentiae" (*ST* I, q. 22, a. 1).

30. *ST* II-II, q. 47, a. 8.

31. "Providentia autem, sicut et prudentia, est ratio in intellectu existens, praeceptiva ordinationis aliquorum in finem" (*ST* I, q. 23, a. 4).

the act of willing an end, but also *synesis* and choice...."[32] This distinction given by the authors between Eternal Law and providence may be understood of the radical source of this obligatory power, which is the Eternal Law, since the very existence of providence comes from the Eternal Law, as we shall see.

As for the second difference noted, i.e., that providence is about singular things, the Eternal Law about the common good, here again we find a distinct disagreement from the explicit words of St. Thomas. Thus: "We must say, however, that all things are subject to divine providence, not only in general, but even in their own individual selves,"[33] an expression that would seem to leave no doubt as to the mind of St. Thomas as he takes the universal nature of providence almost for granted. Again we find: "Since God, then, provides universally for all being, it belongs to His providence to permit certain defects in particular effects, that the perfect good of the universe may not be hindered, for if all evil were prevented, much good would be absent from the universe."[34] This same doctrine is taught expressly in the *Summa Contra Gentiles*.[35]

32. "Providentia...ponitur in actu intellectus, in quo consistit prudentia, nimirum in praecepto et imperio.... Si autem providentia non esset praeceptiva, ac proinde in tali praecepto consisteret, non redderetur a D. Thoma sufficiens ratio ejus, quod dixerat, nimirum providentiam esse in intellectu, atque adeo essentialiter esse actum intellectus praesupponentem voluntatem finis; cumque in sententia ejusdem Doctoris...providentia non solum praesupponat voluntatem finis, sed etiam Synesim [*sic*], et electionem...." (Salmanticenses, *Cursus Theologicus*, Vol. II, *De Praedestinatione* [Paris: Victor Palmé, 1876], Tract. II, Disp. II, Dubium II, §III).

33. "Sed necesse est dicere omnia divinae providentiae subiacere, non in universali tantum, sed etiam in singulari" (*ST* I, q. 22, a. 2).

34. "Cum igitur Deus sit universalis provisor totius entis, ad ipsius providentiam pertinet ut permittat quosdam defectus esse in aliquibus particularibus rebus, ne impediatur bonum universi perfectum" (*ST* I, q. 22, a. 2 ad 2).

35. E.g., *SCG* III, c. 75.

In the *Summa Contra Gentiles* is perhaps the basis of this distinction given by the authors. Here St. Thomas insists that providence extends to the very smallest things, concluding his argument in these words: "His providence applies to all singulars immediately."[36] In the mind of St. Thomas, providence was not restricted to singular things, though it did extend to the smallest; in this latter respect it differed from the Eternal Law which is concerned *only* with the universal.

The third distinction placed between providence and the Eternal Law seems to be the real concept of St. Thomas: the Eternal Law is the general principle, providence is like a conclusion from this principle. We will understand this better if we grasp the basis of this analogy, the other member of which was before the mind of St. Thomas in writing of the Eternal Law. In *De Veritate*, St. Thomas tells us that: "The eternal law should be thought of as existing in God as those principles of action exist in us which we know naturally and upon which we base our deliberation and choice. These belong to prudence or providence."[37] St. Thomas was drawing an analogy between the Natural Moral Law and its precepts, on the one hand, and the Eternal Law and providence on the other. In the Natural Moral Law we have two fundamental general principles—*Bonum est faciendum, malum est vitandum* ["Good is to be done, evil is to be avoided"]—from these are drawn all the other precepts of the Natural Moral Law; so also the Eternal Law is the general principle from which all the ordinations of providence flow.

36. "Eius igitur providentia est omnium singularium immediate" (*SCG* III, c. 76).

37. "Lex enim aeterna est consideranda in Deo, sicut accipiuntur in nobis principia operabilium naturaliter nota, ex quibus procedimus in consiliando et eligendo: quod est prudentiae, sive providentiae" (*De Veritate*, q. 5, a. 1, ad 6).

That this is indeed the sense of St. Thomas can be shown quite clearly. In *De Veritate* we read: "God's providence is not the eternal law; it is something that follows upon the eternal law.... Similarly, the eternal law in God is not His providence, but, as it were, a principle of His providence; for this reason one can, without any inconsistency, attribute an act of providence to the eternal law in the same way that he attributes every conclusion of a demonstration to self-evident principles."[38] The same doctrine can be found in the *Summa Contra Gentiles*.[39]

It may be noted that in the whole tract in the *Summa Contra Gentiles*, St. Thomas insists again and again on this conception of the Eternal Law as the "*ratio providentiae*." In the *Summa Theologiae* itself, throughout all of Question 93 (I-II), St. Thomas repeatedly speaks of the Eternal Law as the "*ratio providentiae*" and the "*ratio gubernationis divinae*." By this he means not only the actual government, in its execution, but also as it exists in the divine mind. Even though we did not have *De Veritate* and *Summa Contra Gentiles* to assure us of this, there are sufficient indications of it in the *Summa* itself. We have already quoted one text quite explicit in this regard; and in this Question 93 itself the minor of an objection reads: "But the type of Divine providence is the eternal law"—a statement which St. Thomas in his response not only concedes but defends.[40]

38. "Dicendum, quod providentia in Deo proprie non nominat legem aeternam, sed aliquid ad legem aeternam consequens.... Et similiter etiam in Deo lex aeterna non est ipsa providentia, sed providentiae quasi principium; unde et convenienter legi aeternae attribuitur actus providentiae, sicut et omnis effectus demonstrationis principiis indemonstrabilibus attribuitur" (*De Veritate*, q. 5, a. 1, ad 6. Cf. ibid., ad 7).

39. *SCG* III, c. 97, c. 115, c. 121, etc.

40. "Sed ratio divinae providentiae est lex aeterna, ut dictum est" (*ST* I-II, q. 93, a. 3, obj. 3 and ad 3).

In answer to another objection he says expressly "the eternal law is the type of Divine providence, as stated above."[41]

St. Thomas then placed the difference between the Eternal Law and providence in the difference between a principle and a conclusion, drawing an analogy with the first principles of the Natural Moral Law and the precepts or conclusions drawn from these principles. But it must be remembered that this is only an analogy, not a strict comparison, for the things are of different orders. It was perhaps the oversight of this fact that led to the statement that providence was concerned only with singular things.

In the *Summa Contra Gentiles* St. Thomas goes even more deeply into this question, determining just in what this basis or principle of divine providence consists. Thus he tells us: "The first principle in providential arrangement is the end; the second is the form of the agent; and the third is the arrangement of the order of the effects" (here St. Thomas adds the caution which we have already quoted).[42] Again he says: "Now, in the aforesaid order, in which the rational Plan of divine providence is observed, we have said that first place is occupied by divine goodness as the ultimate end, which is the first principle in matters of action. Next comes the numerical plurality of things, for the constitution of which there must be different degrees in forms and matters, and in agents and patients, and in actions and accidents. Therefore, just as the first rational principle of divine providence is simply the divine goodness, so the first rational principle in creatures is

41. "Lex aeterna est ratio divinae providentiae, ut dictum est" (*ST* I-II, q. 93, a. 5, ad 3; cf. *ST* I, q. 22, a. 1, ad 1 [explicit]).

42. "Primum ergo principium in dispositione providentiae est finis; secundum, forma agentis; tertium, ipsa dispositio ordinis effectuum" (*SCG* III, c. 80).

their numerical plurality, to the establishment and conservation of which all other things seem to be ordered."[43]

In these two explanations of this very profound question three distinct steps are placed as the root of providence: (a) the divine goodness; (b) the divine form as it is imitable by creatures, or, viewing it differently as in the second quotation, the multitude of creatures who can represent this goodness by imitating the divine form; (c) the disposition of the order of effects. Applying the general principles of law laid down by St. Thomas, as he expressly wished them to be applied when he said "the type in him who governs the acts of his subjects, bears the character of a law, provided the other conditions be present which we have mentioned above,"[44] we can see that in laying down these three principles St. Thomas not only gave the fundamental reasons of providence and concretely determined his notion of the Eternal Law, he also gave the fundamental sources of the Eternal Law itself, probing this question to the very bottom.

As we have shown in the first chapter of this dissertation, law is a dictate or "*imperium*" or precept of the practical reason of one who has care of a perfect community. Applying this first requirement, namely precept of practical reason, we see at once that St. Thomas did not place the Eternal Law in the divine goodness

43. "In praedicto autem ordine, secundum quem ratio divinae providentiae attenditur, primum esse diximus divinam bonitatem, quasi ultimum finem, qui est primum principium in agendis; dehinc vero rerum numerositatem; ad quam constituendam necesse est gradus diversos in formis et materiis, et agentibus et patientibus, et actionibus et accidentibus esse. Sicut ergo prima ratio divinae providentiae simpliciter est divina bonitas, ita prima ratio in creaturis est earum numerositas, ad cuius institutionem et conservationem omnia alia ordinari videntur" (*SCG* III, c. 97).

44. "Ratio gubernantis actus subditorum, rationem legis obtinet, servatis aliis quae supra esse diximus de legis ratione" (*ST* I-II, q. 93, a. 1).

which cannot be called a precept. The same criterion rules out the second principle or the divine form as imitable by creatures. This leaves only the third principle or what St. Thomas calls the "disposition of the order of effects."

Precept or "*imperium*" is an act of prudence which follows counsel and judgment in the reason and election in the will.[45] St. Thomas does not admit counsel in God except in a very broad analogical sense[46] for counsel implies some doubt, some hesitation while all the knowledge of God is infallibly certain. As to the divine judgment and election as bearing on this question he says:

> And so, the fact that God loves His goodness is necessary, but the fact that it is represented by means of creatures is not necessary, because divine goodness is perfect without them. Hence, the fact that creatures are brought into existence, though it takes its origin from the rational character of divine goodness, nevertheless depends solely on God's will. But, if it be granted that God wills to communicate, insofar as is possible, His goodness to creatures by way of likeness, then one finds in this the reason why there are different creatures, but it does not necessarily follow that they are differentiated on the basis of this or that measure of perfection, or according to this or that number of things. On the other hand, if we grant that, as a result of an act of divine will, He wills to establish this particular number of things, and this definite measure of perfection for each thing, then as a result one finds the reason why each thing

45. *ST* II-II, q. 47, a. 8; *ST* I-II, q. 17, a. 1; *ST* I-II, q. 17, a. 3, ad 1.

46. *ST* I, q. 22, a. 1, ad 1.

> has a certain form and a certain kind of matter. And the same conclusion is obvious in regard to the things that follow. So, it becomes apparent that providence disposes things according to a rational plan; yet this plan is taken as something based on the divine will.[47]

The process then, as outlined by St. Thomas would be: (a) the divine goodness as the final end of all things; (b) the divine form showing the ways in which this goodness could be imitated by creatures; (c) the divine will to represent this goodness in creatures, or the will to create; (d) the divine judgment as to the order this representation will take; (e) the divine election of that order; (f) the divine "*imperium*" or precept, following the election and judgment, and commanding that order's establishment and conservation—the "*dispositio ordinis effectuum*" ["arrangement of the order of the effects"].

As is plain from our comparison of the Eternal Law with providence, St. Thomas considered this precept—in which the Eternal Law precisely consists—as general in character. In the

47. "Sic igitur quod Deus suam bonitatem amet, hoc necessarium est: sed hoc non necessario sequitur, quod per creaturas repraesentetur, cum sine hoc divina bonitas sit perfecta. Unde quod creaturae in esse producantur, etsi ex ratione divinae bonitatis originem habeat, tamen ex simplici Dei voluntate dependet. Supposito autem quod Deus creaturis suam bonitatem communicare, secundum quod est possibile, velit per similitudinis modum: ex hoc rationem accipit quod sint creaturae diversae. Non autem ex necessitate sequitur quod secundum hanc vel illam perfectionis mensuram, aut secundum hunc vel illum numerum rerum. Supposito autem ex divina voluntate quod hunc numerum in rebus statuere velit, et hanc unicuique rei perfectionis mensuram: ex hoc rationem accipit quod habeat formam talem et materiam talem. Et similiter in consequentibus patet. Manifestum igitur fit quod providentia secundum rationem quandam res dispensat: et tamen haec ratio sumitur ex suppositione voluntatis divinae" (*SCG* III, c. 97).

*Summa Contra Gentiles*[48] St. Thomas shows at some length how all the diversity of the world is deduced, as conclusions from a principle, from the simple diversity of the forms of creatures. So that it would seem to be sufficient if the eternal precept commanded the diversity of forms of actual things and their direction to the final end, or divine goodness. From this basic principle providence could deduce, by way of conclusion, all its ordinations; for, as St. Thomas says, "the first rational principle in creatures is their numerical plurality, to the establishment and conservation of which all other things seem to be ordered."[49]

From this treatment of the essence of the Eternal Law we see that St. Thomas conceived it as answering exactly and completely to the requirements he would demand of all laws—namely, it is essentially of reason, a precept or "*imperium*" of the practical intellect but supposing the election of the will; at the same time it is the precept of the governor of a perfect community and to the common good.[50] And all this is included in St. Thomas's definition of Eternal Law as "nothing else than the type of Divine Wisdom, as directing all actions and movements."[51]

## V. Scope of the Eternal Law

**1. By Way of Participation.** The scope of the Eternal Law can be considered either from the point of view of participation in or of subjection to that law. Under the first heading comes the

48. Ibid.

49. "Prima ratio in creaturis est earum numerositas, ad cuius institutionem et conservationem omnia alia ordinari videntur" (Ibid).

50. *ST* I-II, q. 90.

51. *ST* I-II, q. 93, a .1.

possibility of this law being known, not in itself, but as regards its rational subjects. From what we have said above it is evident that no one, but God and the blessed who see God as He is in Himself, can know this law directly, that is as it is in itself; since it is in God and really identical with the divine essence. *A fortiori*, no one but God can comprehend it.[52]

The Eternal Law can, however, be known by what St. Thomas calls a participation or irradiation; in this way every rational creature knows this law, at least materially, if not formally under the aspect of law. The profound basis for this statement is that every cognition of truth is a participation of the Eternal Law, for each existing thing has truth only insofar as it imitates the divine intellect; in other words, conforms to the Eternal Law which is the measure of things and is the truth itself.[53]

This proof has a profundity that our exposition of the essence of the Eternal Law allows us to grasp somewhat more easily. St. Thomas gives a thorough exposition of this proof in *De Veritate*. Here he says that truth is to be found in the intellect and in things existing.[†] Truth is found in things inasmuch as they imitate the divine intellect which is "their measure, as art is the measure of all products of art"; and, in another way, inasmuch as they, of their

52. *ST* I-II, q. 93, a. 2, *corp*. and ad 2.

53. *ST* I-II, q. 93, a. 1, ad 3; ibid., a. 2.

† **Editor's Note:** Jan Aertsen has written numerous studies of the nature of truth according to Thomas Aquinas. For example: "Truth as Transcendental in Thomas Aquinas," *Topoi*, Vol. 11 (1992): pp. 159–71; "Truth in Thomas Aquinas," in *Doctor Communis: The Contemporary Debate on the Truth* (Vatican City: Pontifical Academy of St. Thomas Aquinas, 2002), pp. 50–4; "Is Truth *Not* a Transcendental for Aquinas?," in *Wisdom's Apprentice: Thomistic Essays in Honor of Lawrence Dewan, O.P.*, ed. Peter A. Kwasniewski (Washington, DC: The Catholic University of America Press, 2007), pp. 3–12.

very nature, cause a true apprehension in the human intellect, which measures things. Going still deeper, St. Thomas explains: "By its form a thing existing outside the soul imitates the art of the divine intellect; and, by the same form, it is such that it can bring about a true apprehension in the human intellect. Through this form, moreover, each and every thing has its act of existing. Consequently, the truth of existing things includes their entity in its intelligible character, adding to this a relation of conformity to the human or divine intellect."[54] Thus it is the form of the existing thing that is the foundation of its truth both in reference to the divine and to the human intellect; as we have explained above, the essence of the Eternal Law consists precisely in the precept commanding the diverse forms of things. The direct derivation of the truth of actually existing things from the Eternal Law is thus evident; *a fortiori* then, the cognition of this truth is a cognition of the Eternal Law.

That this is the meaning of St. Thomas is brought out more clearly in this same tract in *De Veritate* when he says:

> Natural things from which our intellect gets its scientific knowledge measure our intellect. Yet these things are themselves measured by the divine intellect, in which are

54. "In rebus creatis invenitur veritas in rebus et in intellectu, ut ex dictis patet: in intellectu quidem secundum quod adaequatur rebus quarum notionem habet; in rebus autem secundum quod imitantur intellectum divinum, qui est earum mensura, sicut ars est mensura omnium artificiatorum.... Res autem existens extra animam, per formam suam imitatur artem divini intellectus, et per eandem nata est facere veram apprehensionem in intellectu humano, per quam etiam formam unaquaeque res esse habet; unde veritas rerum existentium includit in sui ratione entitatem earum, et superaddit habitudinem adaequationis ad intellectum humanum vel divinum" (*De Veritate*, q. 1, a. 8).

> all created things—just as all works of art find their origin in the intellect of an artist. The divine intellect, therefore, measures and is not measured; a natural thing both measures and is measured; but our intellect is measured, and measures only artifacts, not natural things. A natural thing, therefore, being placed between two intellects is called true insofar as it conforms to either. It is said to be true with respect to its conformity with the divine intellect insofar as it fulfills the end to which it was ordained by the divine intellect.... With respect to its conformity with a human intellect, a thing is said to be true insofar as it is such as to cause a true estimate about itself.[55]

The words used by St. Thomas must be noted particularly for they bring out clearly the work of the Eternal Law. Thus "the divine intellect, which is their measure,"[56] "natural things...are themselves measured by the divine intellect,"[57] "it is said to be true with respect to its conformity with the divine intellect insofar as it fulfills the end to which it was ordained by the divine intellect."[58]

55. "Res naturales, a quibus intellectus noster scientiam accipit, mensurant intellectum nostrum...sed sunt mensuratae ab intellectu divino, in quo sunt omnia sicut omnia artificiata in intellectu artificis. Sic ergo intellectus divinus est mensurans non mensuratus; res autem naturalis, mensurans et mensurata; sed intellectus noster mensuratus et non mensurans res quidem naturales, sed artificiales tantum. Res ergo naturalis inter duos intellectus constituta, secundum adaequationem ad utrumque vera dicitur; secundum enim adaequationem ad intellectum divinum dicitur vera, in quantum implet hoc ad quod est ordinata per intellectum divinum.... secundum autem adaequationem ad intellectum humanum dicitur res vera, in quantum est nata de se facere veram aestimationem" (*De Veritate*, q. 1, a. 2).

56. "Intellectum divinum, qui est earum mensura" (*De Veritate*, q. 1, a. 8).

57. "Res naturales...mensuratae ab intellectu divino" (*De Veritate*, q. 1, a. 2).

It is the divine intellect, as it is the measure and rule of things, as it is ordinative of things, that is the source of this truth; in other words, it is the divine intellect as it is the Eternal Law.

As a final proof of this we may point out that St. Thomas has employed the very same example here in *De Veritate*[59] that he uses in opening his tract on the Eternal Law: "Just as in every artificer there pre-exists a type of the things that are made by his art, so too in every governor there must pre-exist the type of the order of those things that are to be done by those who are subject to his government."[60]

From this proof it can be concluded that all men know the Eternal Law, at least as regards the first principles of the Natural Moral Law—truths which are universally known. Beyond this, the participation of the Eternal Law under its aspect of knowledge of that Law, varies with the greater or less knowledge of truth, keeping in mind always the distinction of material and formal knowledge of the Eternal Law.[61] This same proof is expressed more simply, though less profoundly, by saying that the Eternal Law can be known by its effects which we can easily see all about us.[62]

Under this same heading of participation falls the derivation of all other laws from the Eternal Law. Taking law formally, as dynamic, moving, directing things to their end, we can see

58. "Secundum enim adaequationem ad intellectum divinum dicitur vera, in quantum implet hoc ad quod est ordinata per intellectum divinum" (ibid.).

59. *De Veritate*, a. 2 and a. 8.

60. "Sicut in quolibet artifice praeexistit ratio eorum quae constituuntur per artem, ita etiam in quolibet gubernante oportet quod praeexistat ratio ordinis eorum quae agenda sunt per eos qui gubernationi subduntur" (*ST* I-II, q. 93, a. 1).

61. *ST* I-II, q. 93, a. 2.

62. *ST* I-II, q. 93, a. 2, ad 1.

clearly the derivation of all law from the Eternal Law. In every series made up of essentially dependent motive agents, the second moves only by the power of the first, all the power of movement possessed by the second mover is derived from the first. Law is a motive agent directing, moving men to an end and the Eternal Law is the first, the supreme law; every law existing besides that Eternal Law derives its power as law from that first supreme law.[63]

This is the same argument as the "*prima via*" ["first way"] of St. Thomas proving the existence of God[64] and like that argument, its whole demonstrative power lies in the understanding of the "series of movers" as being dependent, each upon its immediate superior, not only for its being but for the actual movement itself. That is, the members of the series are dependent "*per se*" not "*per accidens*."[†]

Thus the meaning of St. Thomas is that this ordinative movement towards an end in derived or subordinate laws, such as the Natural Moral Law and human laws, derives its efficacy from a superior ordinative movement which ordains all things to their end. This subordinate ordinative movement that is derived law, in establishing a rule of action, is itself following a higher

63. *ST* I-II, q. 93, a. 3.

64. *ST* I, q. 2, a. 3.

† **Editor's Note:** William Augustine Wallace, O.P., (1918–2015) devoted much profound reflection to the first of Aquinas's "Five Ways." His essays remain very useful. For example: "Physics and God: A Statement and Defense of the *Prima Via* in the Light of Modern Science" (STLr. diss., Pontifical Faculty of the Immaculate Conception, 1954); "Newtonian Antinomies Against the *Prima Via*," *The Thomist*, Vol. 19, No. 2 (1956): pp. 151–92; "The Cosmological Argument: A Reappraisal," *Proceedings of the American Catholic Philosophical Association*, Vol. 46 (1972): pp. 43–57; "The First Way: A Rejoinder," *The Thomist*, Vol. 39, No. 2 (1975): pp. 375–82.

rule; and it is precisely from its adhesion to this higher rule that its efficacy as a law is derived. In more concrete terms: a human law has the "*ratio legis*" only insofar as it is according to right reason[65]; and insofar as it is according to right reason it is following the higher rule of the Natural Moral Law. This latter, a participation of the Eternal Law, is the rule ordaining man's actions to the perfection of his form, consequently to the "*bonum rationis*"; and, as we have already seen, this particular form is the result of the Eternal Law. St. Thomas sums up this teaching very briefly: "An act is called evil in itself [*secundum se*]...when the act is in discord with the rectitude of reason.... And because the natural law is something according to right reason, Augustine therefore says...that an act is called sinful [*peccatum dicitur*] insofar as it is in discord with the eternal law, whose expression is the natural law itself."[66]

We have explained the meaning of St. Thomas here at some length because the words of his argument are open to misinterpretation. Thus taking the idea of movement alone, we might think that St. Thomas was reducing the efficacy of law to the presupposed movement of the will, and from this back to the will of the supreme legislator—a species of voluntarism that would give us a kind of "divine right of legislators," making of law an imposition of will instead of a rule of reason—a notion that is widely accepted today. To get the real sense of St. Thomas we must take his argument without mutilating it. Thus he starts off this proof

65. *ST* I-II, q. 93, a. 3, ad 2.

66. "Actus malus secundum se dicitur...secundum quod actus discordat a rectitudine rationis.... Et quia lex naturalis est secundum quam ratio recta est, ideo Augustinus dicit...quod peccatum dicitur, inquantum discordat a lege aeterna, cujus expressio est ipsa lex naturalis" (*II Sent.*, d. 42, q. 2, a. 5).

by saying: "The law denotes a kind of plan [*ratio*] directing acts towards an end,"[67] i.e., not *any* kind of movement but an *ordinative movement of reason* to an end. From this he argues to a first *movement of reason*. To take only the notion of movement as the basis of the argument would be to destroy the argument altogether, for it would automatically take the notion of law out of the discussion. The point of the argument lies precisely in keeping intact the notion of law, i.e., an ordinative movement towards an end, for the argument is trying to prove that that movement which is law, not any kind of movement is derived from the Eternal Law.

This proof also contains the argument, given by many of the authors, from the fact that a law which is such, not by essence but only by participation, is derived from a law "*per essentiam*," namely the Eternal Law. Billuart notes here that a law might be derived from the Eternal Law as it is the supreme exemplar of all laws; inasmuch as all laws should conform to it; as it is the efficient cause of legislative power; or inasmuch as these laws are really dictated and approved by the Eternal Law through the medium of faith and reason.[68] But these considerations add nothing substantial to the profound explanation of this derivation given by St. Thomas and indeed seem little more than a superficial statement of St. Thomas's profound reasoning.

It should not be concluded from this that all laws bind "*iure divino*" ["by divine right"]. A law binds in this way only because it has God for its immediate author; so that laws coming through

67. "Lex importat rationem quandam directivam actuum ad finem" (*ST* I-II, q. 93, a. 3).

68. Billuart, *Tract. de Legibus*, Diss. II, a. 1 and 2.

the medium of human power do not bind "*iure divino*" though they are derived from the Eternal Law.[69]

**2. By Way Of Subjection.** From our consideration of the essence of the Eternal Law, its subjects are quite evident. The Eternal Law is the divine precept regulating and ordaining all creatures and their actions to the divine goodness; like all law it deals only with the means to the end.[70] Consequently it extends to everything capable of direction to that one end, and to nothing else.[71] Everything that pertains to the divine nature or essence is without the scope of this law; rather it is the law itself.

All created things, necessary or contingent, are subject to the Eternal Law, though in different ways. The necessary and natural contingent things cannot be subjects of law in a strict sense, i.e., subjects of a moral law, since they are not rational, are not capable of rights and duties. Necessary things have the very reason for their necessity from the Eternal Law[72]; contingent things are contingent in the sense that they proceed from secondary causes which are capable of being impeded in their action, and this by ordination of the Eternal Law. Even the actual failure of these causes to produce their effects is the result of the Eternal Law, the law of the Universal Governor. Thus they are contingent, not in regard to the Eternal Law or the first cause, but in respect to human laws and the immediate secondary cause of these contingent things.[73]

69. Ibid.
70. *ST* II-II, q. 47, a. 8; *ST* II-II, q. 50.
71. *ST* I-II, q. 93, a. 4.
72. *ST* I-II, q. 93, a. 4, ad 4.
73. *ST* I-II, q. 93, a. 5, ad 3.

In subjecting these natural things to the Eternal Law, St. Thomas is using the term "law" in a broad analogical sense for the purpose of indicating that everything is subject to divine direction. A human legislator by his precept imprints something, so to speak, on the mind of his subjects which is the principle of action of these subjects as such, that is the "*verbum mentale*" is imprinted on the minds of men as the result of the promulgation of the law. In governing the world, God imprints on the whole of creation the natural principles which govern the proper actions of every individual nature.[74]

This is the basis of St. Thomas's analogy; but it is only an analogy as he himself makes abundantly clear. Thus in giving the analogy he uses such phrases as "God is said to command the whole of nature.... Consequently irrational creatures are subject to the eternal law, through being moved by Divine providence; but not, as rational creatures are, through understanding the Divine commandment."[75] Further on in the tract we find a clear cut distinction between participation of law "*per modum cognitionis*" ("by way of knowledge") and "*per modum actionis et passionis*" ("by way of action and passion"), in which latter way alone, i.e., in a purely passive manner, irrational creatures can be said to be subjects of law.[76] In the *Summa Contra Gentiles* we find the explicit statement: "Since law is simply a certain rational plan and rule of operation, it is fitting that law be given only to those

74. *ST* I-II, q. 93, a. 5.

75. "Per hunc modum dicitur Deus praecipere toti naturae.... Unde alio modo creaturae irrationales subduntur legi aeternae, inquantum moventur a divina providentia, non autem per intellectum divini praecepti, sicut creaturae rationales" (*ST* I-II, q. 93, a. 5). Cf. ibid., ad 1 and ad 2.

76. *ST* I-II, q. 93, a. 6.

beings who know the rational character of their work. Now, this is proper only to a rational creature. Therefore, it was appropriate that law was given to the rational creature only."[77]

It is then quite clear that St. Thomas limited law in its strict sense to rational creatures alone; it is also clear that in his *ex professo* treatment of law in the *Summa Theologiae* he maintained this same distinction, not only from the texts we have already cited but from the prologue to the very first question on law[78] where he tells us: "God...instructs us by means of His Law" and of course it is only rational creatures who are capable of instruction in this strict sense. In treating of the Eternal Law this distinction was not overlooked or confused; but using terms that would admit of no misunderstanding, St. Thomas treated the Eternal Law, both in its strict sense and its wider sense, giving the whole tract a unity otherwise impossible, yet avoiding any confusion.

The manner in which men are subject to the Eternal Law is really the subject matter of our fourth chapter—on the Natural Moral Law. It may be summed up here briefly by saying that men are subject to this law in its broad sense, insofar as they have instincts and instinctive acts, "*actus hominis*" ("act of a human being"); over and above this they are subject to it in a way peculiar to themselves, i.e., rationally, for they have a knowledge of the law, as we have shown. And this last is subjection to the Eternal Law in the strict sense, taking the law as a moral law. In this sense the subjection of men to this law extends to their human acts,

77. "Cum lex nihil aliud sit quam quaedam ratio et regula operandi, illis solum convenit dari legem qui sui operis rationem cognoscunt. Hoc autem convenit solum rationali creaturae. Soli igitur rationali creaturae fuit conveniens dari legem." (*SCG* III, c. 114).

78. "Deus, qui et nos instruit per legem" (*ST* I-II, q. 90, prolog.).

good or bad, for all these acts are subject to divine government. This is true not only of the acts themselves but also of their consequences, for which men must suffer the penalties imposed by that law or enjoy the rewards established by it, not only in this life but for eternity.[79]

79. *ST* I-II, q. 93, a. 6; ibid., ad 3.

* * *

# Chapter III

## Doctrine of Suárez

It will be useful, for a good understanding of the Thomistic doctrine on law, to consider well the teaching of Suárez on this question. Suárez is the chief opponent of the Thomistic teaching within the Church and his notion is quite directly opposed to that of the Thomists so that the contrast of one with the other will make both stand out much more clearly. Then too the Suárezian doctrine has received wide acceptation, perhaps as much because of the thoroughness of the exposition from an historical and positive point of view as from the doctrine itself. We shall give as clear an explanation as possible of Suárez's teaching on Law, on the Eternal Law, and on the Natural Moral Law, offering a criticism of the first two immediately; the Natural Moral Law according to Suárez will be criticized at the end of our last chapter. In the course of these criticisms we shall point out the chief points of opposition to the doctrine of St. Thomas.

* * *

## I. Essential Notion of Law

**1. Exposition.** Taking law in its strict sense—as moral law—Suárez says it is evident that it pertains only to an intellectual creature since it essentially implies moral direction and the intellectual creature alone is capable of this. Moreover it pertains to the mind of that intellectual nature, taking "mind" as including both intellect and will, for it is by the mind that the intellectual nature is capable of moral direction to an end. All this quite evidently refers to the subject of law; but from this it follows *a fortiori* that law, as it is in the legislator, pertains to the mind.[1]

Narrowing the question still further, Suárez finds that law not only pertains to the mind but to some act (*actus secundus*) of that mind. The reason for this further determination is that law has the proximate power of binding its subjects and of moving them; this power cannot exist in a habit or potency, except radically and remotely. Again, "*imperium*" and "*ordinare*" express the notion of act and it is by law that these are constituted ("*fiunt*").[2]

To determine the exact nature of this "*actus secundus*," the author considers law in its different phases. As it is in some outward sign, for example a code of laws, it is quite evident that law consists in some exterior act, such as the written or spoken word which manifests the mind of the legislator. This exterior act includes not only the act itself but also the term of that act.[3] As it is in its subject, law—or this act in which law consists—is merely a judgment of the intellect, proposing and proximately applying the law to the will. An act of the will is unnecessary here,

1. Suárez, *De Legibus*, lib. I, c. 4, no. 2.
2. Ibid., no. 3.
3. Ibid., no. 4.

for law precedes the will of the subject and obliges it.[4] Here the word "act" would not seem to include the term of the act or the "*verbum expressum*" ("expressed word") of the mind. In treating of the exterior act, Suárez says expressly that by "act" he includes the term of that act; but here he makes no such statement, but says without qualification "with respect to law as it may exist in its human subject, such law unquestionably consists in an act of the mind, and of itself requires only a judgment by the intellect and not an act of the will."[5]

Law, then, as it is in some outward sign consists in an external act; as it is in the subject, in the judgment of the intellect. Taking law in its most proper sense, as it is in the legislator, we find that several acts are involved. The first of these is an act of the will intending or willing the common good of governing subjects well.[6] This is followed by an act of counsel in the intellect as to which law is just, and convenient to the end in view. This act of the intellect does not, of course, follow successively in God as it does in man, for in God there is no succession. These two acts, of will and of intellect, are the remote foundation of law.[7]

Following counsel is an act of judgment on the part of the intellect by which the legislator establishes and discerns that such

4. Ibid., no. 5.

5. "Praetera de lege, prout esse potest in homine legi subjecto, certum est consistere in actu mentis, et per se solum requirere judicium intellectus et non actum voluntatis" (ibid. [p. 57]). **Editor's Note:** Unless otherwise noted, English translations of Suárez's texts are taken from Francisco Suárez, *Selections from Three Works*, ed. Thomas Pink, trans. Gwladys L. Williams et al. (Indianapolis: Liberty Fund, 2015). The page numbers of this translated edition are included at the end of references in brackets.

6. Ibid., no. 6.

7. Ibid.

a disposition of things will be for the good of the community and that it is expedient that this disposition be observed by all. It is this act that gives law its rational character; by it law is prudently and rationally framed.[8] This act of judgment is followed immediately by an act of election on the part of the will by which the legislator accepts the judgment of the intellect, chooses it and wills that it be observed by his subjects.[9] *In this act of election precisely consists the essence of law*: "With regard to the essence of the matter, a more intelligible and more easily defensible assertion is this: law in its mental aspect (so to speak), as it exists in the lawmaker himself, is the act of a just and upright will, the act whereby a superior wills to bind an inferior to the performance of a particular deed."[10]

Essentially this act of the will does not deal with the actual execution of the law but with the obligation of its subjects; it is a will to oblige those subjects and without it there would be no obligation.[11] No act of the intellect is required after this act of the will to make up the essence of law; indeed an act of the intellect by way of "*imperium*" or command is impossible.[12] All that is required to make the law complete is that it be manifested to the subjects by some outward sign.[13] To accomplish this end, more intellectual acts are assigned, but these all follow the law essentially constituted; thus we have a judgment of the intellect

8. Ibid., c. 4, no. 6.

9. Ibid., no. 7.

10. "Spectando ad rem ipsam melius intelligi, et facilius defendi, legem mentalem (ut sic dicam) in ipso legislatore esse actum voluntatis justae et rectae, quo superior vult inferiorem obligare ad hoc vel illud faciendum" (Suárez, *De Legibus*, lib. I, c. 5, no. 24 [p. 81]). Cf. Ibid., no. 8; ibid., ch. 4, no. 10ff.

11. Suárez, *De Legibus*, lib. I, c. 4, no. 8.

12. Ibid., no. 11.

13. Ibid., no. 12.

concerning this manifestation and an act of the will putting this judgment into execution.[14]

The basis of the exclusion of any "*imperium*" on the part of the intellect following the election of the will—in which law precisely consists—is the notion of the part played by the intellect in the individual man. Thus the particular potency, which is to execute the "*imperium*" or command within the individual himself, does not perceive the force of this command (says Suárez) nor does it pertain to the intellect to apply the potency to operation, but only to propose an object to the will; it is the task of the will to apply the other potencies to actual operation. This notion of "*imperium*" in the individual is extended to the "*imperium*" concerning other individuals, or the "*imperium*" of the governor. This is cited as the more common opinion and supposed from *Summa Theologiae* I-II, q. 17, a. 1.[15]

We now have a clear notion of Suárezian doctrine on law. In its most strict sense—as it is in the legislator—law consists in an act of the will, election, which is preceded by counsel and judgment on the part of the intellect, and of course by the act of the will choosing the end. But it is this election of the will which is essentially and *per se* law.

In proof of this explanation of law, Suárez offers no less than eight or nine arguments, citing in his favor all those theologians who hold that "*imperium*" is an act of the will as against the Thomistic teaching that it is an act of the intellect.[16] Passing over the argument from authority, i.e., on the grounds that Scripture and the civil

14. Ibid., no.14.

15. Ibid., no.11 and no. 12.

16. Ibid., c. 5, no. 8.

codes call the will of God and of a prince law,[17] we find five principal arguments from the properties of law itself. These arguments proceed from the fact that: law is a rule and measure of action[18]; that law enlightens and directs the subject[19]; that law ordains to an end[20]; that law has power to move and apply the subject to the exercise of the act[21]; and that law has the power to oblige.[22]

In other details of law, Suárez agrees substantially with St. Thomas. Law is framed by public authority[23] for the common good[24] and is perpetual[25]; promulgation is of the essence of external law, i.e., law as it exists outside of the legislator as opposed to law as it is in the legislator.[26] The same four acts are assigned to law[27] and the same end.[28] Coming down to a definition Suárez says: "law 'is a common, just and stable precept, which has been sufficiently promulgated.'"[29] By "*commune preceptum*" he includes the notion of public authority making the law since it is for the whole community. In this phrase he places the essence of law in a precept but, as we have seen, by a precept he understands an act of the will; specifically, election. And it may be noted here that

17. Ibid., no. 9.
18. Ibid., no. 11.
19. Ibid., no. 12.
20. Ibid., no. 13.
21. Ibid., no. 15.
22. Ibid.
23. Ibid., c. 8, no. 2.
24. Ibid., c. 7.
25. Ibid., c. 10.
26. Ibid., c. 11, no. 3.
27. Ibid., c. 15, no. 2.
28. Ibid., c. 13, no. 3.
29. "Lex est commune praeceptum, justum ac stabile, sufficienter promulgatum" (ibid., c. 12, no. 5 [p. 142]).

under this act its term is not included as it was under the first aspect of law, namely as it is in an outward sign where it included the written record.

**2. Criticism.** The opposition between the doctrines of Suárez and St. Thomas, while evident enough, is not always grasped in its entirety. For purposes of clarity, brevity, and completeness we give that opposition in graphic form.

LAW AS IT IS IN THE LEGISLATOR

| St. Thomas | Suárez |
|---|---|
| 1. Consists in "*imperium*" or precept. | 1. Consists in "*imperium*" or precept. |
| 2. Which is essentially an act of reason. | 2. Which cannot possibly be an act of reason. |
| 3. This act of reason presupposes an act of the will. | 3. "*Imperium*" is essentially of the will; no consequent act of reason pertains to essence of law. |
| 4. This act of reason includes the term of this act or the proposition of reason. | 4. This act of the will does not include its term. |
| 5. Since reason is the cause of the precept it is the cause of its corollary or obligation. | 5. The will to oblige the subjects is the sole cause of obligation; without it there would be no obligation. |
| 6. The notion of ordination, of regulation is primary in law; that of obligation, while essential, is derivative from notion of precept. | 6. Notion of obligation is primary since it is in the act of the will to oblige subjects that law essentially consists. |

With these two expositions of law clearly understood, it is necessary for a judgment of them to examine proofs adduced for each one. We have already seen the arguments which St. Thomas uses to prove his opinion; it remains only for us to examine those of Suárez.

(A) The Question of "*Imperium*." Examining these arguments of Suárez we see that they can all be stated in a single sentence: "*imperium*" is an act of the will, not of the intellect. And this is exactly the fundamental difference between Suárez and St. Thomas. All the properties advanced by Suárez as proofs that law is an act of the will are given by St. Thomas as properties of "*imperium*."[30] To determine the value of these arguments we must determine the potency which elicits the act of "*imperium*."

According to St. Thomas the acts of the mind preceding "*imperium*" are: counsel and judgment in the intellect, followed by election on the part of the will. Then comes "*imperium*" on the part of the intellect commanding the thing chosen by the will; this in turn is followed by "*usus*" of the will or the actual application to the potencies executing the "*imperium*."[31]

"*Imperium*" according to Thomists, is made up of three elements: ordination, intimation, and motion. The first two of these acts are acts of the intellect, as is plain from the ordinary concept of the soul. It is the work of the intellect to compare objects, to determine the better of two or more (in a word to reason) and to propose these objects to the will and to the other potencies. As regards ordination, plainly it is of the intellect for it is attributed to intellectual virtues such as wisdom, prudence,

30. *ST* I-II, q. 17, a. 1; *ST* II-II, q. 47, a. 8; ibid., q. 50.

31. *ST* I-II, q. 13 seq. Ibid., q. 17, a. 3, ad 1; *ST* II-II, q. 47, a. 8.

art, etc.; moreover whatever order is found in natural or voluntary things is of the intellect; works of nature are works of intelligence, while in voluntary things the will follows the order of reason, whether that order be true or false. The third element in "*imperium*"—motion—is caused by the will which is the first mover "*ad exercitium*" ("to exercise"); but it proceeds immediately from the intellect which participates in the motion of the will just as the election of the will participates in the rational judgment that precedes it.[32]

An act which proceeds from two potencies, as does "*imperium*" is elicited by, is essentially from, the potency which gives substance to the act; the potency in which the act is consummated. The substance and material of "*imperium*" is not motion; but rather ordinative and intimating motion. Motion is rather the form than the substance. The classic example of this is the act of martyrdom. The motive power behind it is charity. It is is from charity that the exercise of the act proceeds; but it is the virtue of fortitude that gives substance to the act, that receives this motion from charity and consummates the act. And martyrdom is the elicited act of fortitude.[33]

The reasons for placing these acts of intellect and will ("*imperium*" and "*usus*") after election are based on experience; on the fact that there is a great difference in electing or choosing to do a thing and the actual execution of that election. On the

32. *ST* I-II, q. 17, a. 1; Cajetan in I-II, q. 17, a. 1; John of St. Thomas, *Cursus Theologicus*, Disp. VII, a. 2, no. 6, no. 7, no. 14; (in I-II, q. 8, a. 17) Charles-René Billuart, O.P., *Summa Sancti Thomae Hodiernis Academiarum Moribus Accommodata*, Vol. 4, *De Actibus Humanis*, Diss. II, a. 7, a. 2.

33. *ST* I-II, q. 13, a. 1; Cajetan, in I-II, q. 17, a. 1; John of St. Thomas, *Cursus Theologicus*, Disp. VII, a. 2, no. 8, no. 9, no. 14, no. 34; *ST* I-II, q. 17, a. 1, ad 1.

part of the will there is the work of the potencies and faculties in the actual execution, the resistance of the appetite and external impediments—all of which election, being a purely internal act, did not have to deal with. These new inconveniences and difficulties did not hinder the election; indeed, they could not appear until after it. Consequently they demand a new effort, a new efficacy of motion and application from the part of the will (*usus*); and that this new motion might not be blind but reasonable, a new ordination of reason is necessary to direct it and to deal with these new elements. It is necessary to resort to another tribunal in which the executions themselves will be finally judged and ordained according to this ultimate individuation and these new circumstances. Since it is a question of execution, an intimation of this ordination is *a fortiori* required by the executive potencies. This ordination and intimation is the work of "*imperium.*"[34]

According to Suárez these last two acts are unnecessary. The judgment preceding the election is sufficient to make the election reasonable, while the force of the election carries to act to completion; "*imperium,*" with all that it implies, is wholly from the will, is contained in the election itself. That "*imperium*" is necessary we believe is evident from the preceding paragraph. But Suárez maintains that any "*imperium*" of the intellect is not only unnecessary but impossible after election because the potency involved could not perceive this "*imperium*" and the intellect has only to propose an object to the will, not to apply the potencies to actual operation.

34. John of St. Thomas, *Cursus Theologicus*, Disp. VII, a. 1, no. 7, and no. 9. Billuart, *De Actibus Humanis*, Diss. I.

John of St. Thomas calls this statement of the impossibility of intellectual "*imperium*" ridiculous[35] and St. Thomas himself answers it.[36] The will is indeed blind, but it is not necessary for the will or any other potency to understand in order to be moved by the intellect any more than it is necessary for the feet to see in order that a man walk in a certain direction. Just as the physical members operate, not for themselves, but for the whole man, so it is with the potencies of the soul. To be more specific, the intellect moves the will by proposing an object to it; the sensitive faculties are moved by the intellect through the medium of imagination whose apprehension is subordinate to and moved by reason. From the imagination is regulated the sensitive appetite which in turn regulates the members of the body. As for the actual exercise, the intellect moves these faculties by the movement in which it participates from the will.[37]

To Suárez's contention that the will enlightens and directs the subject, is a measure of human actions, and ordains to an end—all properties of "*imperium*"—we need only refer to Cajetan's comment quoted above, for all these qualities are reduced to ordination and intimation.

What would seem to be Suárez's strongest arguments are that the "*imperium*" as an act of reason cannot have moving power and cannot oblige. To meet this difficulty it is necessary to remember that "*imperium*" does not consist in mere motion or mere obligation, but in motion and obligation as ordaining things to an end and as manifesting this ordination—both of which elements

35. John of St. Thomas, *Cursus Theologicus*, Disp. VII, a. 15.

36. *ST* I-II, q. 17, a. 5, ad 2.

37. John of St. Thomas, *Cursus Theologicus*, Disp. VII, a. 1, no. 15.

are supplied by the intellect.[38] Moreover, "*imperium*," according to the Thomistic conception, though essentially an act of the reason, is not exclusively so but presupposes and includes an act of the will.[39] While it is true that the intellect of itself could only move the will and the other potencies as regards specification, by proposing an object to them, "*imperium*" of the reason moves not only as regards specification but also as regards "*exercitium*," here and now to be done, because of its nature it includes an efficacious movement of the will. It participates in the preceding election of the will.[40]

It would be just as correct to say that election cannot be reasonable, cannot choose with discretion, because election is an act of the will while judgment is an act of the intellect, as to say that the "*imperium*" of reason lacks motive power since it is not of the will. Just as the election participates in the preceding judgment of the intellect and thus is reasonable, so "*imperium*" participates the preceding election of the will and so is motive or obligatory. The will, though the first principle of motion in man, can move nothing, neither as regards the potencies immediately subject to it, nor as regards other individuals, except by means of an intimation denouncing and directing what the will wishes to be done. This directive intimation and denunciation is the material, the substantial element in "*imperium*" and is the work of reason. So that although from the point of view of movement to

38. Cajetan in I-II, q. 17, a. 1; John of St. Thomas, *Cursus Theologicus*, Disp. VII, a. 2, no. 17 and no. 28.

39. *ST* I-II, q. 17, a. 1; and Cajetan's commentary on this article.

40. *ST* I-II, q. 17, a. 1; and John of St. Thomas, *Cursus Theologicus*, Disp. VII, a. 1, no. 13.

41. John of St. Thomas, *Cursus Theologicus*, Disp. VII, a. 2, no. 28 and no. 32.

actual exercise of an act and in its origin, "*imperium*" begins from the will, it is materially, substantially, and immediately from the intellect.[41]

## II. The Eternal Law

**1. Exposition.** Suárez distinguishes two states of the Eternal Law: an internal state, the law as constituted in God, the Legislator; and an external state, when it was proposed to creatures.[42] In the first sense it is certainly eternal, as are all things in God. In the second sense it is not less certainly not eternal since it is coexistent with creatures.[43] As to the objection that the Eternal Law could not be promulgated from eternity, he agrees with the answer of St. Thomas that actual promulgation is not necessary but it suffices that promulgation on the part of the legislator is from eternity.[44] The reason for this, in the theory of Suárez, is that the decree of God is immutable; consequently, as regards the consummation of law, this is peculiar to Eternal Law alone for the the decree of human legislators is mutable. Consequently before promulgation it is rather the determination to frame a law than the law itself which is in the mind of the legislator.[45]

In scope the Eternal Law does not touch the acts of the divine intellect and will as they regard God.[46] Taking the Eternal Law as a moral law, it does not extend to irrational but only to rational

42. Suárez, *De Legibus*, lib. II, c. 1, no. 5.
43. Ibid.
44. Ibid., no. 11.
45. Ibid.
46. Ibid., lib. II, c. 2, no. 2 and no. 9.

creatures.[47] All moral acts are the material of this law either by way of precept or prohibition.[48]

Determining the essential notion of this law, Suárez says it is eternal and is in the mind of God.[49] Moreover it consists in some act ("*actus secundus*"); and this "*actus secundus*" is a free act.[50] Eternal Law is not a mere idea[51] but necessarily demands an act of the will because liberty is formally in the will.[52] Eternal Law does not consist in any act of the intellect preceding the decree of the divine will.[53] *It does consist precisely in a free decree of the divine will establishing an order to be observed*, whether we take this law in a broad sense as reaching to all creatures, or strictly as the moral law binding intellectual creatures alone.[54]

As proof of this explanation of the Eternal Law, Suárez says that the Eternal Law in its broad sense, as it directs irrational creatures and those acts of man which are not moral, is evidently in the will of God because God commands these things immediately and proximately, not by speaking but by making them such as they are.[55] That Eternal Law, taken as a moral law, is in the will of God, is proved by the same arguments which were given to prove that all law is precisely an act of the will.[56]

47. Ibid., no. 13.
48. Ibid., no. 15.
49. Ibid., lib. II, c. 3, no. 1.
50. Ibid., no. 3.
51. Ibid.
52. Ibid., no. 4.
53. Ibid., no. 5.
54. Ibid., no. 6.
55. Ibid., no. 7 and no. 8.
56. Ibid., no. 8.

**2. Criticism.** Since every explanation of the Eternal Law in God is merely an application of our method of understanding to the action of God, a criticism of such an explanation must be nothing more than a criticism of the basic notion of law. If that basic notion is erroneous, then *a fortiori* its application to God is erroneous. As a result, our criticism of Suárez's notion of law is an effective refutation of Eternal Law; particularly as he uses the same arguments in its behalf as he used to prove his idea of law in general. As for the argument adduced here in favor of the Eternal Law in its broad sense, it is based on the idea that any "*imperium*" of the intellect is merely a sign, a manifestation of an "*imperium*" of the will. It can therefore be reduced to the basis of all Suárez's arguments, namely that "*imperium*" is in the will, not in the intellect; we have already dealt with this contention in criticizing Suárez's doctrine on law in general.

One point worth mentioning here because it is usually emphasized in comparing the Thomistic doctrine with that of Suárez, is brought out clearly in the exposition of Eternal Law we have just given from the latter. When Suárez, in explaining the response to the objection on the promulgation of the Eternal Law, says that before promulgation it is rather a proposal or determination to frame a law than the law itself that is in the mind of the human legislator, he brings out what many others have termed the "active" element of his doctrine in contrast to the "passive" nature of Thomistic doctrine. The term is not only misleading, for both are decidedly active, but quite incorrect. Suárez includes under the term "act," in which law consists, the term of that act; but this is true only of the law as it is in some outward sign. As it is in the subjects it is precisely the act of judgment. As it is in the legislator the term of the act is not included. It is an act of the will and such an act does not have its term in the will itself; so that if we are to place the essence of law in the will we cannot include this "term" in the essential nature of law. On the contrary, the Thomistic teaching is that it is precisely in this term of the act of the intellect—the proposition—that law consists. It is evident at once that both these conceptions are active, since both are held to be precepts. The difficulty is really a corollary of the basic difficulty as to the origin of "*imperium*," whether it is an act of the intellect or the will.

## III. The Natural Moral Law

**1. Exposition.** In treating of the Natural Law, Suárez is speaking of law under a different aspect than that taken in his tract on law in general and on the Eternal Law. There he was speaking of law as it is in the legislator; here he is treating of law as it is in the subject. Natural Moral Law, as it is in the legislator, is nothing less than the Eternal Law itself.[57]

Taken in this light, i.e., as it is in the subject, we may distinguish a double element in the Natural Moral Law. The first is human nature itself, the rational essence inasmuch by reason of this essence some things are naturally convenient to it, others inconvenient or opposed to it. In this way human nature is the foundation of natural honesty.[†] The second element is the power of human nature to discern the difference between the convenient and the inconvenient, the suitable and unsuitable; this is

57. Ibid., c. 5, no. 14.

† **Editor's Note:** Farrell is using "honesty" in the sense Aquinas uses the word "*honestas*." Cf. *ST* II-II, q. 145.

the Natural Moral Law itself, commanding or prohibiting things to the human will.[58]

This general notion of Natural Moral Law—namely that it is in the human reason—is in perfect accord with Suárez's general tract on law where he held that law in its subjects is a judgment of reason.[59] This agreement with his general tract is complete when he declares that the Natural Moral Law is an "*actus secundus*" of human reason, namely judgment; this does not seem to include the term of this act—the proposition—for he says, "I have no doubt but that, it is in the actual judgment of the mind that natural law, in the strictest sense, exists."[60] But he would also admit that the natural light of reason can be called the Natural Moral Law, for even when men do not think or judge, the Natural Moral Law is retained in their hearts. In other words this "*lumen naturale*" ("natural light") can be considered as the Natural Moral Law permanently within man, though most properly speaking the judgment of the intellect is the Natural Moral Law.[61]

Suárez further clarifies this notion of the Natural Moral Law by saying that this law is not only indicative of good and evil, it also contains a precept of good and a prohibition of evil.[62] Natural Law therefore is that "*imperium*" which can induce an obligation; and since the human judgment cannot do this, it must merely show an obligation that is already supposed. So this judgment,

58. Ibid., no. 9.

59. Ibid., lib. I, c. 4, no. 5.

60. "Non dubito, quin in actuali judicio mentis propriissime existat lex naturalis" (ibid., lib. II, c. 5, no. 14 [p. 205]).

61. Ibid.

62. Ibid., c. 6, no. 5.

inasmuch as it has the "*ratio legis*," indicates an "*imperium*" from which the whole obligation proceeds,[63] namely the divine "*imperium*". This judgment of the natural reason indicating what is good or bad "*per se*" for man, indicates that these things are according to the will of God and are to be done, or contrary to that will and are to be avoided.[64]

This will is in God as supreme governor and is the will to oblige his subjects.[65] This will of God to oblige his subjects is not the whole reason for the good and evil which is in the observation of that Natural Moral Law or its violation. It supposes in these acts a certain necessary honesty or malice and to this joins a special divine obligation.[66] The Natural Moral Law is a true and proper divine law whose author is God. The obligation added by the Natural Moral Law to the natural goodness or malice of an act is from the divine will.[67]

This statement of Suárez regarding a presupposed or natural honesty and malice in human acts, brings up the difficulty of "necessary morality." In the hypothesis that God never commanded or prohibited the things of the Natural Moral Law, they would still be good or evil.[68] Suárez answers that from this we can only conclude that a certain goodness or malice of human acts does not consist formally in their discord or accord with any law or precept. They are evil but are not prohibited in this hypothesis. Besides, it must be remembered, the "natural"

63. Ibid., no. 6.
64. Ibid., no. 8.
65. Ibid., no. 9.
66. Ibid., no. 11.
67. Ibid., no. 13.
68. Ibid., no. 14.

goodness and malice and that proceeding from the precept of the Natural Moral Law cannot actually be separated.[69]

Yet these acts would be morally evil, since they are free acts, solely on account of discord with right reason, without a law. In answer to this objection Suárez makes some astonishing statements. He says a human act has goodness or malice from its object precisely considered as it harmonizes or does not harmonize with right reason. From this aspect it can be called evil, a sin and culpable without reference to a proper law. Besides this culpability, a human act has a special reason of good or evil, "*in ordine ad Deum*" ("in order/relation to God") added by divine law. In this second way a human act is called sin or "*culpa apud Deum*" ("guilt in the sight of God") in a special way, by reason of a transgression of the law.[70]

He adds that it is in this way St. Thomas distinguishes sin as against reason and as an offense against God in *Summa Theologiae* I-II, q. 71, a. 6, ad 5.[71] Thus he, Suárez, says in this case of an act being against reason, the act would be morally evil, a sin and culpable, not however theologically, "*in ordine ad Deum*."[72] Natural Moral Law truly prohibits everything that is *per se* evil or inordinate in human acts; without this prohibition these acts would not have ("*ut sic dicam*" ["so to speak"]) the consummate and perfect "*ratio culpae et offensae divinae*" ("character...of guilt and of an offence against God").[73] As a final answer we may say

69. Ibid., no. 15.
70. Ibid., no. 17.
71. Ibid., no. 18.
72. Ibid.
73. Ibid., no. 19 [p. 226].

that this hypothesis is altogether impossible for God could not refrain from prohibiting what is intrinsically evil and commanding what is intrinsically good.[74]

Having established the divine nature of this law and the obligation it imposes, Suárez determines the part played by the judgment of human reason—in which the Natural Moral Law precisely consists. It is a sign of the divine will, it is sufficient promulgation of the will of God and no other is needed to make up the notion of law. The reason for this is not only because the judgment of reason manifests the inconvenience or convenience of these acts, but also because it shows man that the inconvenient acts displease the author of nature, as the supreme Lord and Provider and Governor of this same nature.[75]

The material of this law is "*bonum ex se honestum*" ("good which is essentially honest") and its opposite; it embraces all the precepts, or moral principles, which have an evident honesty necessary to moral rectitude so that their opposites contain a moral inordination or malice. This is the only law that supposes goodness and malice; other laws make this moral goodness and malice by their statues.[76]

This material can be divided into three classes: (a) First principles, such as "*Honestum est faciendum, pravum vitandum*" ("one must do good, and shun evil"), "*Quod tibi fieri non vis alteri ne feceris*" ("do not to another that which you would not wish done to yourself") and so on; (b) more determined and particular precepts yet still "*per se nota*" ("self-evident") e.g., "*Justitia*

74. Ibid., no. 21.

75. Ibid., no. 24.

76. Ibid., c. 7, nos. 1–4.

*est servanda*" ("justice must be observered"), "*Deus est colendus*" ("God must be worshipped"), etc.; (c) Deductions from these principles, either easily arrived at such as "adultery is evil," or not easily known by all, as "fornication is intrinsically evil," "a lie is never justified," etc.[77]

As characteristics of this law Suárez points out that it is one; that it is universal as to time and subjects, though in the latter respect we must distinguish the law "*in actu primo*" (light of the intellect) and "*in actu secondo*" (actual judgment of the intellect). As regards the light or the intellect, the law is absolutely universal; as regards the actual judgment it is universal at least as regards the first principles.[78]

This law cannot be abolished from the hearts of men and holds for all states of men[79]; it obliges in conscience[80] and every obligation in conscience is in some way, at least mediately and remotely, the effect of the Natural Moral Law.[81] Punishment does not properly pertain to this law because, although guilt is incurred by its transgression, natural reason cannot define that punishment, so that the quality or quantity of punishment does not properly speaking follow from the "*imperium*" of any mere natural law. The guilt or "*reatus*" rather follows from the natural and intrinsic condition of the fault or "*culpa*" so that although the punishment is not determined by the Natural Moral Law, the offender can be punished according to the judgment of a

77. Ibid., no. 5 [p. 235].

78. Ibid., c. 8, nos. 5 and 6.

79. Ibid., nos. 6 and 8.

80. Ibid., c. 9, no. 2.

81. Ibid., no. 11 seq.

competent judge. Permission has no place in this law because it deals only with the essentially good and evil.[82]

The Natural Law is intrinsically immutable, both in general and in particular as long as there remains rational nature with the use of reason and liberty.[83] This does not of course exclude addition to that law for these are not strictly speaking changes of the law, since the law as it existed before these additions still remains intact.[84] When St. Thomas and Aristotle say that some precepts of the Natural Moral Law are changed or cease to exist or suffer exception "*in paucioribus*" ("in some few cases"), they are speaking of change improperly taken, through a mere extrinsic denomination, by reason of the change in the material. Precepts are of two kinds: those which suffer no change either in themselves or in their material, such as the general principles; the other class consists of those which allow of change in the material with which they deal. It is concerning these latter that it is said they are changed or allow exceptions. The precept, considered in itself, allows of no exception; it seems to in these cases because it has not been sufficiently stated.[85]

Although all the precepts of the Natural Moral Law are immutable, they are not all equally known. This law cannot be completely erased from the minds of men, but men can remain in ignorance of some of its precepts though it is likely that no one precept is unknown to all men. What one man or one nation is ignorant of, is known by some other individual or nation and *vice versa*.[86]

82. Ibid., c. 12, 1.
83. Ibid., c. 13, 2.
84. Ibid., no. 1.
85. Ibid., no. 7.
86. Ibid., no. 10.

**2. Criticism.** The criticism of Suárez's explanation of Natural Moral Law will be found at the end of the last chapter of this book.

* * *

# Chapter IV

## The Natural Moral Law

In our consideration of the Natural Law we are limiting ourselves strictly to the Natural Moral Law; the Natural Law in the sense of physical laws, or the laws governing irrational animals, is without the scope of our discussion.[†] It is necessary, in commencing our study of the Natural Moral Law, to notice also the distinction between the subjective and objective aspect of this law. This distinction was given by St. Thomas at the very beginning of his tract on law[1] and is repeated in almost the same words at the beginning of his tract on Natural Moral Law: "Law, being a rule and measure, can be in a person in two ways: in one way, as in him that rules and measures; in another way, as in that which is ruled and measured, since a thing is ruled and measured insofar as it partakes of the rule or measure."[2]

This distinction is indeed self-evident from St. Thomas's doctrine on law in general for it states merely that law, existing in the legislator, has its correlative in the subject. In the first case it is reason ruling; in the second it is reason ruled. That there is another aspect of the objective law—namely the order established by law as it is in the legislator and in the subject—is also self-evident.

The objective Natural Moral Law, i.e., as it exists in the legislator, is nothing more than a part of the Eternal Law itself.[3] The Natural Moral Law subjectively considered is found in man himself, in his participation or subjection to the Eternal Law.[4] The order established by this law as it exists in God and as it is participated in by man, is the order of man to his end and to the means by which that end is to be attained. This is so easily perceived that it is passed over by St. Thomas in his tract on the Natural Law. Every law of its very nature, which is to ordain, establishes an order to the end of the law and to the means to that end; as the end of the Eternal Law is the direction of the universe to its final end, quite evidently, in its application to man, it establishes such an order. We find this order mentioned expressly in *Summa Contra Gentiles*: "Now, God has imposed on men's acts a certain order in relation to the final good, as is evident from preceding statements. So, it must be, if this order is rightly laid down, that those who proceed according to this order will attain the final

† **Editor's Note:** See the Introduction for an explanation of how the physical laws and laws governing irrational animals integrate into the natural moral law.

1. *ST* I-II, q. 90, a. 1, ad 1.
2. "Lex, cum sit regula et mensura, dupliciter potest esse in aliquo, uno modo, sicut in regulante et mensurante; alio modo, sicut in regulato et mensurato, quia inquantum participat aliquid de regula vel mensura, sic regulatur vel mensuratur" (*ST* I-II, q. 91, a. 2). Cf. *ST* I-II, q. 91, a. 2, ad 1; and q. 90, a. 3, ad 1.
3. *ST* I-II, q. 91, a. 2, *corp.* and ad 1.
4. *ST* I-II, q. 91, a. 2.

good, and this is to be rewarded; but those who depart from this order by means of sin must be cut off from the final good, and this is to be punished."[5]

## I. The State of the Question

The subject matter of this chapter is exclusively the Natural Moral Law subjectively considered. We have already treated the objective Natural Law, i.e., as it is in the legislator, in explaining the Eternal Law; the objective Natural Moral Law, understood as the order established by that law, is a self-evident conclusion given the Eternal Law and its subjects. Our object then will be to discover what the Natural Moral Law is in man; to get some essential notions of this law within man.

Because of the examples used to illustrate the nature of this Natural Moral Law, e.g., an illumination, radiation, reflection, impression of the Eternal Law, it is sometimes thought that the Natural Moral Law considered as found in man himself is not strictly speaking the law itself. Rather it is an effect of the participation of the Eternal Law, not the participation itself. To determine accurately the subject matter of this chapter we must analyze some of these examples.

The first of these examples calls the Natural Law an *illumination*, a radiation, a reflection from the Eternal Law.[6] In this

5. "Deus autem imposuit actibus hominum ordinem aliquem in respectu ad finem boni, ut ex praedictis patet. Oportet igitur quod, si ordo ille recte positus est, quod incedentes per illum ordinem finem boni consequantur, quod est praemiari: recedentes autem ab illo ordine per peccatum, a fine boni excludi, quod est puniri" (*SCG* lib. III, c. 140).

6. *ST* I-II, q. 93, a. 2; Prümmer, *Manuale Theologiae Moralis*, Vol. I, p. 105, fn 17.

example the Eternal Law would be considered as a great light playing upon the interior of man, as the sun plays upon things exteriorly. This would light up all that interior, enabling man to see what was to be seen; in other words, allowing man to use his power of sight. But it would not contribute to the things to be seen in any objective sense. That is, the things to be seen would have to be there before, or at least concomitantly with the illumination and independent of it taken formally as illumination. If we suppose that in man there is a chart drawn up containing the plan of action he must follow to reach his end; that in man there is also the power to see and understand this chart; then the illumination coming, enables him to see and understand this chart. The question then would be: what part does this illumination play in the Natural Law? It does not seem to be the essence, for it rather supposes the essence, which man sees by its help. Rather it is a "*conditio sine qua non*" of the law.

This is taking illumination in its strictest sense; but it is quite probable that theologians, in using this example, did not understand it in just this way. Their meaning most probably was: this illumination, coming from God, enlightens man in a superior way, furnishing him not only with light but also with the order which he must see and observe. Taken in this sense we find three elements in this example: (a) the illumination strictly so-called, i.e., the application of the Eternal Law to men; (b) the light and order, i.e., that portion of Eternal Law which is applied to men; (c) the effect of this illumination in man. The problem is to determine which of these constitutes the essence of the Natural Moral Law. As the second example is slightly more tangible and the problem remains the same, we will examine the second example before commenting on this first one.

As a second example the Natural Moral Law is said to be an *impression* of or participation of the Eternal Law.[7] We can best analyze this example by reducing it to everyday terms. Take a definite seal or stamp and with it stamp a bit of warm wax. In this supposition we have three elements: (a) the seal itself, or the things to be impressed; (b) the actual impression of these things, or the act of the hand pressing the seal upon the wax; (c) the effect of this impression on the wax.

In the case of the Natural Moral Law, with which we are dealing, these elements could be resolved into: (1) the seal itself—that part of the Eternal Law which is moral, i.e., which is to be applied to man, in contrast to the whole scope of the Eternal Law governing the universe; (2) the actual application of this seal—the application of this portion of the Eternal Law to man; (3) the effects of this impression—the perpetuation of the seal in man, the image of the seal remaining permanently.

Examining the first of these three elements, we see at once that it cannot answer to the requirements of the essence of the subjective Natural Moral Law; at least this is not what we mean by the subjective side of this law. It is rather what we have already explained in our second chapter, it is strictly in God and is nothing more than a part of the Eternal Law considered apart from the rest.

The second elements—the actual impression of the portion of the Eternal Law applicable to men—may perhaps answer to the requirements of the essence of the Natural Moral Law. It answers most closely to the descriptions of the law given by theologians, taking the terms of these descriptions in the strictest sense; for

7. *ST* I-II, q. 91, a. 2; ibid., q. 106, a. 1, ad 2; *Supplem.* q. 65, a. 1.

this is strictly "impression." Then too, it makes no presuppositions; it carries the whole content of the law with it. But St. Thomas, in his general tract on law[8] said that law can be of only two kinds; to this our daily use of the word adds a third: (a) as law is in the legislator; (b) as it is in the subject; (c) as it is in some external sign, such as a code of laws, which is really nothing more than a kind of permanent promulgation. Now this actual impression is certainly not in God, the legislator, but rather comes from him. Neither is it in the subject, man, otherwise it would be the third element or the effects of the actual impression. Nor is it in some external sign, such as a book or some other means of promulgation. Rather it would seem to be a law "*in transitu*," on its way from the legislator to the subject. This becomes more apparent when we consider that an act of God, such as this actual impression, is executed instantaneously and without the use of an instrument, so that this actual impression can be reduced to a divine precept.

The third element—the effect of this impression in man—has the serious objection against it that it is after all an effect. It is certainly not the law as it is in the legislator; no less certainly is it not law as law is in an external sign, such as a book. But it does answer to some of the requirements for law as it is in the subject. If every law, considered as it is in the subject, is really an effect, the difficulty against this third element will be more or less answered.

Taking the example of human laws, to clarify this last statement, we have the following results. A human law, framed by the legislator, is the efficient cause of the effect it produces in the

8. *ST* I-II, q. 90, a. 1, ad 1; ibid., a. 3, ad 1; ibid., q. 91, a. 2.

subject; and that effect is nothing more than the act of reason, by which the subject comprehends the law, and the resulting proposition of reason making this comprehension permanent.[9] And this is exactly law considered as it is in the subject.

In the Natural Moral Law we have a somewhat parallel case. The legislator, God, frames the Eternal Law; this Eternal Law, applied to man, has a very definite effect on man, its subject—an effect far more reaching than the effect of a human law for its permanency and accuracy is ensured by much more stable means than a mere proposition of reason.[10]

It is also to be noted that this third element of which we are speaking can be called "illumination" or "impression"; thus we say: "this impression is good or bad," meaning that the effect left by the seal on wax is or is not a perfect reproduction of the original seal. This third element also makes no presuppositions, as it is the image, the reproduction of the original seal, carrying with it the whole content of the law.

This, then, will be the object of our investigation: to determine just what these effects of the Eternal Law applied to man are, i.e., what is the Natural Moral Law in man.

## II. Existence of the Natural Moral Law

The existence of the Natural Moral Law could be proved from authority, for example from the Epistle to the Romans, where St. Paul says: "For when the Gentiles, who have not the law, do by nature those things that are of the law; these having not

9. *ST* I-II, q. 93, a. 5.

10. Ibid.

the law are a law to themselves: Who show the work of the law written in their hearts, their conscience bearing witness to them, and their thoughts between themselves accusing or also defending one another."[11] Or it could also be proved from the authority of the Fathers, for example, St. Ambrose and St. Augustine.[12] But Catholics, to whom these proofs would carry conviction, have no need of proofs, they have that characteristic of freely admitting the truths proposed and approved by common sense. And, as will be apparent from the few rational arguments we will offer, the existence of the Natural Moral Law is indeed a truth of the common sense of mankind, taking this term in its most proper, its scholastic sense.

Because of the intimate connection between the Natural Moral Law and the Eternal Law, the most obvious proof of the existence of the former is drawn from the existence of the latter. Thus it is self-evident that the Eternal Law exists and is effectively applied to creatures. Indeed this is the only explanation of the order present in the world, an order whose presence every advance of experimental science only confirms. Since the Natural Moral Law, as it is in the legislator, is a part of the Eternal Law—namely the part to be applied to men, *a fortiori* the Natural Moral Law, as it is in the legislator, exists. The Natural Moral Law as it is in the subjects of that law, i.e., in men, is nothing more than the effects of the application of the Eternal Law. Since the Eternal Law is effectively applied, *a fortiori* these effects exist in men.[13]

11. Rom. 2:14–16
12. Cf. Billuart, *Tract. de Legibus*, Diss. II, a. 2.
13. *ST* I-II, q. 91, a. 2.

Proceeding from the effects, instead of from the source of these effects, the existence of the Natural Moral Law is no less evident. The reason of every man, independently of positive laws and indeed previous to them, declares that some actions are bad and must be avoided, while others are good and must be done. Since this is precisely the work of moral law, i.e., to regulate human actions, to be the rule of those actions, commanding the good and forbidding the bad, it is evident that there is a moral law intimately present to every man. This law we call the Natural Moral Law.[14] Nor is this testimony of conscience an unconscious projecting of Christian morality into the purely natural field, a generalization of what we ourselves know because of our Catholic heritage. This testimony of conscience as to the existence of the Natural Moral Law, is vouched for by such Greek philosophers as Plato, Socrates, Aristotle, and Zeno[15]; while among the Romans we find Cicero, Horatius, Tacitus, Juvenal, not only admitting this law from the testimony of conscience, but extolling it.[16]

A third argument, this time explicitly from the order of the world, and proceeding by way of analogy, clearly shows the unreasonableness of the denial of the Natural Moral Law. The universe, which is ordained to an end, is made up of irrational and rational creation. Both of these, being things created, are therefore defectible and need guidance, direction to attain their end and the end of the universe. Since the irrational creation is guided to its end,

14. Cf. Billuart, *Tract. de Legibus*, Diss. II, a. 2.

15. Cf. Bernard Roland-Gosselin, *La Doctrine Politique de S. Thomas D'Aquin* (Paris: M. Rivière, 1928), p. 4.

16. Cf. Prümmer, *Manuale Theologiae Moralis*, p. 106, no. 152.

and thus to the end of the universe, by natural laws in consonance with the diverse irrational natures, it is, to say the very least, fitting that man also be guided to his end and to the end of the universe, by a natural law in consonance with his rational nature, i.e., by a natural moral law.[17]

## II. Essence of the Natural Moral Law

Looking through the works of St. Thomas, we find three different explanations of the essence of this law, seemingly contrary one to the other. The first of these places the law in the natural inclinations of man: "Wherefore it [the rational creature] has a share of the Eternal Reason, whereby it has a natural inclination to its proper act and end: and this participation of the eternal law in the rational creature is called the natural law."[18] This same notion of the Natural Moral Law is repeated and emphasized time and time again, for instance:

> Now just as man, by such pronouncement, impresses a kind of inward principle of action on the man that is subject to him, so God imprints on the whole of nature the principles of its proper actions. And so, in this way, God is said to command the whole of nature.... And thus all actions and movements of the whole of nature are subject to the eternal law. Consequently irrational creatures are subject to

17. Cf. Prümmer, ibid.

18. "Unde et in ipsa [creatura rationalis] participatur ratio aeterna, per quam habet naturalem inclinationem ad debitum actum et finem. Et talis participatio legis aeternae in rationali creatura lex naturalis dicitur" (*ST* I-II, q. 91, a. 2). Cf. obj. 2 and ad 2.

> the eternal law, through being moved by Divine providence; but not, as rational creatures are, through understanding the Divine commandment.[19]

This seems to say that the law was the inclinations, since the government of man by the Eternal Law is the Natural Moral Law, and reason merely recognized this law.[†] In the *ex professo* tract on the Natural Moral Law we find such as the following: "all those things to which man has a natural inclination, are naturally apprehended by reason as being good, and consequently as objects of pursuit, and their contraries as evil, and objects of avoidance. Wherefore according to the order of natural inclinations, is the order of the precepts of the natural law."[20] "To the natural law belongs everything to which a man is inclined according to his nature. Now each thing is inclined naturally to an operation that is suitable to it according to its form: thus fire is inclined to give heat. Wherefore, since the rational soul is the proper form of man, there is in every man a natural inclination to

---

19. "Sicut autem homo imprimit, denuntiando, quoddam interius principium actuum homini sibi subiecto, ita etiam Deus imprimit toti naturae principia propriorum actuum. Et ideo per hunc modum dicitur Deus praecipere toti naturae.... Et per hanc etiam rationem omnes motus et actiones totius naturae legi aeternae subduntur. Unde alio modo creaturae irrationales subduntur legi aeternae, inquantum moventur a divina providentia, non autem per intellectum divini praecepti, sicut creaturae rationales" (*ST* I-II, q. 93, a. 5).

† **Editor's Note:** The opening of this sentence has been adjusted for readability. The original text takes the quotation from Aquinas as part of the sentence, and Farrell begins his subsequent analysis thus: "as if to say the law was the inclinations...".

20. "Omnia illa ad quae homo habet naturalem inclinationem, ratio naturaliter apprehendit ut bona, et per consequens ut opere prosequenda, et contraria eorum ut mala et vitanda. Secundum igitur ordinem inclinationum naturalium, est ordo praeceptorum legis naturae" (*ST* I-II, q. 94, a. 2).

act according to reason: and this is to act according to virtue."[21] Again: "There are two ways in which a thing may be instilled into man. First, through being part of his nature, and thus the natural law is instilled into man."[22]

The second of these explanations, the one favored by Billuart,[23] seems to place the Natural Moral Law in the light of reason itself, i.e., in the intellectual potency or faculty before its actual operation.[24] St. Thomas makes direct reference to this in treating *ex professo* of the Natural Law when he says: "the light of natural reason, whereby we discern what is good and what is evil, which is the function of the natural law, is nothing else than an imprint on us of the Divine light. It is therefore evident that the natural law is nothing else than the rational creature's participation of the eternal law."[25] In other parts of the *Summa Theologiae* this idea is brought out very strongly, e.g.: "Now it is from the eternal law, which is the Divine Reason, that human reason is the rule of the human will, from which the human derives its

21. "Dictum est enim quod ad legem naturae pertinet omne illud ad quod homo inclinatur secundum suam naturam. Inclinatur autem unumquodque naturaliter ad operationem sibi convenientem secundum suam formam, sicut ignis ad calefaciendum. Unde cum anima rationalis sit propria forma hominis, naturalis inclinatio inest cuilibet homini ad hoc quod agat secundum rationem. Et hoc est agere secundum virtutem" (*ST* I-II, q. 94, a. 3). Cf. Ibid., a. 4.

22. "Dupliciter est aliquid inditum homini. Uno modo, pertinens ad naturam humanam, et sic lex naturalis est lex indita homini" (*ST* I-II, q. 106, a. 1, ad 2). Cf. Ibid., q. 94, a. 2, ad 2; *IV Sent.* d. 33, q. 1, a. 1; *III Sent.* d. 37, q. 1, a. 1, ad 3; *V Ethic*, lect. 12.

23. *Tract. de Legibus*, Diss. II, a. 2, Dico 2.

24. *ST* I, q. 12, a. 2 (definition of "*lumen rationis*").

25. "Quasi lumen rationis naturalis, quo discernimus quid sit bonum et malum, quod pertinet ad naturalem legem, nihil aliud sit quam impressio divini luminis in nobis. Unde patet quod lex naturalis nihil aliud est quam participatio legis aeternae in rationali creatura" (*ST* I-II, q. 91, a. 2).

goodness. Hence it is written (Ps. 4): 'Many say: Who showeth us good things? The light of Thy countenance, O Lord, is signed upon us': as though to say: 'The light of our reason is able to show us good things, and guide our will [the precise end of law], insofar as it is the light (i.e., derived from) Thy countenance.'"[26†] "Although the eternal law is unknown to us according as it is in the Divine Mind: nevertheless, it becomes known to us somewhat, either by natural reason which is derived therefrom as its proper image; or by some sort of additional revelation."[27] "The material sun sheds its light outside us; but the intelligible Sun, Who is God, shines within us. Hence the natural light bestowed upon the soul is God's enlightenment, whereby we are enlightened to see what pertains to natural knowledge; and for this there is required no further knowledge, but only for such things as surpass natural knowledge."[28] In St. Thomas's earlier treatment

---

26. "Quod autem ratio humana sit regula voluntatis humanae, ex qua eius bonitas mensuretur, habet ex lege aeterna, quae est ratio divina. Unde in Psalmo IV, dicitur, multi dicunt, quis ostendit nobis bona? Signatum est super nos lumen vultus tui, domine, quasi diceret, lumen rationis quod in nobis est, intantum potest nobis ostendere bona, et nostram voluntatem regulare [the precise ends of law], inquantum est lumen vultus tui, idest a vultu tuo derivatum" (*ST* I-II, q. 19, a. 4). This same text is quoted and the same interpretation is given in *ST* I, q. 88, a. 3, ad 1; *In Psalm*, IV, 5; *De Veritate* q. 16, a. 3.†

† **Editor's Note:** The bracketed phrase "the precise ends of law" appears in parentheses in the original text.

27. "Licet lex aeterna sit nobis ignota secundum quod est in mente divina; innotescit tamen nobis aliqualiter vel per rationem naturalem, quae ab ea derivatur ut propria eius imago; vel per aliqualem revelationem superadditam" (*ST* I-II, q. 19, a. 4, ad 3).

28. "Sol corporalis illustrat exterius; sed sol intelligibilis, qui est Deus, illustrat interius. Unde ipsum lumen naturale animae inditum est illustratio Dei, qua illustramur ab ipso ad cognoscendum ea quae pertinent ad naturalem cognitionem. Et ad hoc non requiritur alia illustratio, sed solum ad illa quae naturalem cognitionem excedunt" (*ST* I-II, q. 109, a. 1, ad 2).

of this subject, in the *Commentary on the Books of Sentences*, this explanation is given expressly: "The interior law is the light of reason itself, by which we discern what we should do, and whatever in human actions is consonant with this light is totally right [*totum est rectum*]. That which, however, is contrary to this light, is unnatural and evil for man."[29]

The third explanation given by St. Thomas places the Natural Moral Law in the result of an act of the practical reason, i.e., in the proposition of reason. Thus we find: "in the practical reason something that holds the same position in regard to operations, as, in the speculative intellect, the proposition holds in regard to conclusions. Such like universal propositions of the practical intellect that are directed to actions have the nature of law. And these propositions are sometimes under our actual consideration, while sometimes they are retained in the reason by means of a habit."[30] That this remark does not refer only to law as it is in the legislator is evident from the following in the tract on Natural Moral Law: "the natural law is something appointed by reason, just as a proposition is a work of reason."[31]

In *Summa Theologiae* q. 91 we find this significant remark: "Now among all others, the rational creature is subject to Divine

29. "Lex enim interior est ipsum lumen rationis, quo agenda discernimus: et quidquid in humanis actibus huic lumini est consonum, totum est rectum; quod autem contra hoc lumen est, homini est innaturale et malum" (*II Sent.*, d. 42, q. 1, a. 4, ad 3).

30. "Ideo est invenire aliquid in ratione practica quod ita se habeat ad operationes, sicut se habet propositio in ratione speculativa ad conclusiones. Et huiusmodi propositiones universales rationis practicae ordinatae ad actiones, habent rationem legis. Quae quidem propositiones aliquando actualiter considerantur, aliquando vero habitualiter a ratione tenentur" (*ST* I-II, q. 90, a. 1, ad 2).

31. "Dictum est enim supra quod lex naturalis est aliquid per rationem constitutum, sicut etiam propositio est quoddam opus rationis" (*ST* I-II, q. 94, a. 1).

providence in the most excellent way, insofar as it partakes of a share of providence, by being provident both for itself and for others,"[32] and it is only by the *use* of his reason that man provides either for himself or for others. In this same article we find a more explicit statement: "Even irrational animals partake in their own way of the Eternal Reason, just as the rational creature does. But because the rational creature partakes thereof in an intellectual and rational manner, therefore the participation of the eternal law in the rational creature is properly called a law, since a law is something pertaining to reason, as stated above. Irrational creatures, however, do not partake thereof in a rational manner, wherefore there is no participation of the eternal law in them, except by way of similitude."[33]

In the tract on Natural Moral Law we find this interpretation referred to again and again, for example: "All the inclinations of any parts whatsoever of human nature, e.g., of the concupiscible and irascible parts, insofar as they are ruled by reason, belong to the natural law..."[34] "Although reason is one in itself, yet it directs all things regarding man; so that whatever can be ruled by reason,

32. "Inter cetera autem rationalis creatura excellentiori quodam modo divinae providentiae subiacet, inquantum et ipsa fit providentiae particeps, sibi ipsi et aliis providens" (*ST* I-II, q. 91, a. 2). This same point is found more expressly in *SCG* III, c. 78.

33. "Quod etiam animalia irrationalia participant rationem aeternam suo modo, sicut et rationalis creatura. Sed quia rationalis creatura participat eam intellectualiter et rationaliter, ideo participatio legis aeternae in creatura rationali proprie lex vocatur, nam lex est aliquid rationis, ut supra dictum est. In creatura autem irrationali non participatur rationaliter, unde non potest dici lex nisi per similitudinem" (*ST* I-II, q. 91, a. 2, ad 3).

34. "Omnes inclinationes quarumcumque partium humanae naturae, puta concupiscibilis et irascibilis, secundum quod regulantur ratione, pertinent ad legem naturalem" (*ST* I-II, q. 94, a. 2, ad 2). Cf. ibid., *corp.*

is contained under the law of reason."[35] It must be noted that only by an act of reason and the resulting proposition, namely "*imperium*" and precept, does the reason regulate and ordain. Again we find: "Wherefore, since the rational soul is the proper form of man, there is in every man a natural inclination to act according to reason: and this is to act according to virtue. Consequently, considered thus, all acts of virtue are prescribed by the natural law: since each one's reason naturally dictates to him to act virtuously"[36]—i.e., this law consists in a dictate or precept of reason. In this same question this idea is repeated more strongly: "As, in man, reason rules and commands the other powers, so all the natural inclinations belonging to the other powers must needs be directed according to reason. Wherefore it is universally right for all men, that all their inclinations should be directed according to reason."[37]

Frequent reference is also made to this explanation in other parts of the *Summa*, e.g.: "We cannot know the things that are of God [among which is the Eternal Law], as they are in themselves; but they are made known to us in their effects, according to Rm. 1:20: 'The invisible things of God...are clearly seen, being

35. "Ratio, etsi in se una sit, tamen est ordinativa omnium quae ad homines spectant. Et secundum hoc, sub lege rationis continentur omnia ea quae ratione regulari possunt" (*ST* I-II, q. 94, a. 2, ad 3).

36. "Unde cum anima rationalis sit propria forma hominis, naturalis inclinatio inest cuilibet homini ad hoc quod agat secundum rationem. Et hoc est agere secundum virtutem. Unde secundum hoc, omnes actus virtutum sunt de lege naturali, dictat enim hoc naturaliter unicuique propria ratio, ut virtuose agat" (*ST* I-II, q. 94, a. 3).

37. "Sicut ratio in homine dominatur et imperat aliis potentiis, ita oportet quod omnes inclinationes naturales ad alias potentias pertinentes ordinentur secundum rationem. Unde hoc est apud omnes communiter rectum, ut secundum rationem dirigantur omnes hominum inclinationes" (*ST* I-II, q. 94, a. 4, ad 3).

understood by the things that are made.'"[38†] The word to be noted in the preceding text is *intellecta*, i.e., understood, or a completed act of the reason. Again: "the natural law is nothing else than a concept naturally instilled into man, whereby he is guided to act in a befitting manner in his proper actions."[39] This same doctrine is insisted upon in the other works of St. Thomas,[40] but it would serve no purpose to multiply the texts already cited. This third explanation is also the one favored by many theologians.[41]

Though we find these three explanations in St. Thomas, our problem, in searching for the essential notion of Natural Moral Law, is not to choose any particular one of them. An attentive reading of St. Thomas shows that he did not consider these three mutually exclusive. In fact, as can be seen from some of the texts we have already given, he frequently mentions two or even all three of these explanations of the law in the same article. For instance:

---

38. "Ea quae sunt Dei [among which is the Eternal Law], in seipsis quidem cognosci a nobis non possunt, sed tamen in effectibus suis nobis manifestantur, secundum illud Rom. I, invisibilia Dei per ea quae facta sunt, intellecta, conspiciuntur" (*ST* I-II, q. 93, a. 2, ad 1). Cf. ibid., a. 5.

† **Editor's Note:** The bracketed phrase "among which is the Eternal Law" appears in parentheses in the original text.

39. "Lex ergo naturalis nihil aliud est quam conceptio homini naturaliter indita qua dirigitur ad convenienter agendum in actionibus propriis" (*Supplem.* q. 65, a. 1).

40. E.g., *I Sent.*, d. 39, q. 2, a. 2, ad 4; *III Sent.*, d. 37, q. 1, a. 3; *IV Sent.*, d. 33, q. 1, a. 1; *SCG* III, c. 78, etc.

41. E.g., Sylvius in I-II, q. 94, a. 1; Suárez (for act, not proposition), *De Legibus*, lib. II, c. 5, no. 14. Among the moderns, Dom Odon Lottin, O.S.B., "Le droit naturel chez saint Thomas et ses prédécesseurs," *Ephemerides Theologicae Lovanienses*, Vol. 2 (1925): p. 358; Lehu, *Philosophia Moralis*, p. 239.

> Wherefore, since all things subject to Divine providence are ruled and measured by the eternal law…it is evident that all things partake somewhat of the eternal law, insofar as, namely, from its being imprinted on them, they derive their respective inclinations to their proper acts and ends [from this, man is not excluded]. Now among all others, the rational creature is subject to Divine providence in the most excellent way, insofar as it partakes of a share of providence, by being provident both for itself and for others [and of course it is only by the use of his reason that man provides for himself or for others—third explanation]. Wherefore it has a share of the Eternal Reason, whereby it has a natural inclination to its proper act and end [first explanation]: and this participation of the eternal law in the rational creature is called the natural law. Hence the Psalmist after saying (Ps. 4:6): "Offer up the sacrifice of justice," as though someone asked what the works of justice are, adds: "Many say, Who showeth us good things?" in answer to which question he says: "The light of Thy countenance, O Lord, is signed upon us": thus implying that the light of natural reason, whereby we discern what is good and what is evil, which is the function of the natural law [second explanation], is nothing else than an imprint on us of the divine light. It is therefore evident that the natural law is nothing else than the rational creature's participation of the eternal law.[42†]

42. "Unde cum omnia quae divinae providentiae subduntur, a lege aeterna regulentur et mensurentur…manifestum est quod omnia participant aliqualiter legem aeternam, inquantum scilicet ex impressione eius habent inclinationes in proprios actus et fines [from this, man is not excluded]. Inter cetera autem rationalis creatura excellentiori quodam modo divinae providentiae subiacet,

Very often St. Thomas mentions the natural inclinations and the dictate or proposition of reason as making up the Natural Moral Law, not making explicit mention of the light of reason, as it is, *a fortiori*, presupposed in the proposition of reason. Thus treating of the Eternal Law, St. Thomas says God impressed on all nature (thus including rational nature) the principles of the proper actions of each nature; and in this way all nature is subject to the Eternal Law, i.e., by way of natural inclination. Irrational creatures are subject to the Eternal Law inasmuch as they are moved passively by divine providence; but they are not subject to this law through the comprehension of a divine precept, i.e., by a proposition of reason, as are rational creatures.[43] Again, in this tract on the Eternal Law, we have the explicit joining of two of these explanations of the Natural Moral Law. St. Thomas gives the distinction of subjection to the Eternal Law "by way of knowledge; secondly, by way of action and passion, i.e., by partaking of the eternal law by way of an inward motive principle." He then

inquantum et ipsa fit providentiae particeps, sibi ipsi et aliis providens [and of course it is only by the use of his reason that man provides for himself or for others—third explanation]. Unde et in ipsa participatur ratio aeterna, per quam habet naturalem inclinationem ad debitum actum et finem [first explanation]. Et talis participatio legis aeternae in rationali creatura lex naturalis dicitur. Unde cum Psalmista dixisset, sacrificate sacrificium iustitiae, quasi quibusdam quaerentibus quae sunt iustitiae opera, subiungit, multi dicunt, quis ostendit nobis bona? Cui quaestioni respondens, dicit, signatum est super nos lumen vultus tui, domine, quasi lumen rationis naturalis, quo discernimus quid sit bonum et malum, quod pertinet ad naturalem legem [second explanation], nihil aliud sit quam impressio divini luminis in nobis. Unde patet quod lex naturalis nihil aliud est quam participatio legis aeternae in rationali creatura" (*ST* I-II, q. 91, a. 2).

† **Editor's Note:** The bracketed phrases inserted throughout this quotation appear in parentheses in the original text.

43. *ST* I-II, q. 93, a. 5.

says that rational creatures are subject to the Eternal Law in both ways: i.e., by the natural inclinations and by the cognitive act of reason.[44]

This same combination of these different elements runs through the tract on the Natural Moral Law, e.g.: "All those things to which man has a natural inclination, are naturally apprehended by reason as being good, and consequently as objects of pursuit, and their contraries as evil, and objects of avoidance. Wherefore according to the order of natural inclinations, is the order of the precepts of the natural law."[45] "To the natural law belongs everything to which a man is inclined according to his nature. Now each thing is inclined naturally to an operation that is suitable to it according to its form: thus fire is inclined to give heat. Wherefore, since the rational soul is the proper form of man, there is in every man a natural inclination to act according to reason: and this is to act according to virtue. Consequently, considered thus, all acts of virtue are prescribed by the natural law: since each one's reason naturally dictates [precept or proposition of reason] to him to act virtuously."[46†] "As, in man, reason rules and commands the other

44. "Duplex est modus quo aliquid subditur legi aeternae, ut ex supradictis patet, uno modo, inquantum participatur lex aeterna per modum cognitionis; alio modo, per modum actionis et passionis, inquantum participatur per modum principii motivi" (*ST* I-II, q. 93, a. 6).

45. "Omnia illa ad quae homo habet naturalem inclinationem, ratio naturaliter apprehendit ut bona, et per consequens ut opere prosequenda, et contraria eorum ut mala et vitanda. Secundum igitur ordinem inclinationum naturalium, est ordo praeceptorum legis naturae" (*ST* I-II, q. 94, a. 2).

46. "Ad legem naturae pertinet omne illud ad quod homo inclinatur secundum suam naturam. Inclinatur autem unumquodque naturaliter ad operationem sibi convenientem secundum suam formam, sicut ignis ad calefaciendum. Unde cum anima rationalis sit propria forma hominis, naturalis inclinatio inest cuilibet homini ad hoc quod agat secundum rationem. Et hoc est agere secundum virtutem. Unde secundum hoc, omnes actus virtutum sunt de lege

powers, so all the natural inclinations belonging to the other powers must needs be directed according to reason. Wherefore it is universally right for all men, that all their inclinations should be directed according to reason."[47]

It would seem, then, that St. Thomas placed the Natural Moral Law, not in any one of these three, but in all three taken somehow collectively. A glance at the articles in which St. Thomas treats of the essence of this law makes this point of view quite certain. Thus in *Summa Theologiae* question 91, the question of the existence of the Natural Moral Law is proved briefly from the existence of the Eternal Law; the rest of the article is an exposition of the nature of this law in man, what it consists of in the rational creature.[48] And here we have explicit mention of the inclinations, the light of reason and the result of the act of reason or the proposition, as we have already shown. In the first article of q. 94, where St. Thomas is treating *ex professo* of the essence of this law, he places it unequivocally in the result of the act of reason or the proposition. Then in his response to the "*Sed Contra*," which in this case is an objection, he says that a boy cannot use the Natural Law, which is within him habitually, "*propter defectum aetatis*" ("on account of the deficiency of age")—which is true of the light of reason and of the natural inclinations, but is certainly not true of the proposition

naturali, dictat [precept or proposition of reason] enim hoc naturaliter unicuique propria ratio, ut virtuose agat" (*ST* I-II, q. 94, a. 3).

† **Editor's Note:** The bracketed phrase "precept or proposition of reason" appears in parentheses in the original text.

47. "Sicut ratio in homine dominatur et imperat aliis potentiis, ita oportet quod omnes inclinationes naturales ad alias potentias pertinentes ordinentur secundum rationem. Unde hoc est apud omnes communiter rectum, ut secundum rationem dirigantur omnes hominum inclinations" (*ST* I-II, q. 94, a. 4, ad 3).

48. *ST* I-II, q. 91, a. 2.

of reason, for this would be sheer Platonism. In the third article of this same question (*ST* I-II, q. 94, a. 3), we find a third exposition of the essence of this law and here again we see mentioned the natural inclinations of man and the dictate of reason.

If then, as seems certain, St. Thomas placed the essence of the Natural Moral Law in these three elements, namely the natural inclinations, the light of reason, and the proposition of reason, taken in some way collectively, this should be apparent from his classic definition of the Natural Moral Law. This definition reads: "The natural law is nothing else than the rational creature's participation of the eternal law."[49] Examining the terms of this definition we see that we are familiar with the notion of the Eternal Law; we may reasonably suppose a general notion of the meaning of rational creature. The whole content of the definition, from our point of view, lies in the meaning St. Thomas attached to "participation."

This term itself and the ordinary meaning attached to it are well known to all students of scholastic philosophy and theology. The treatment of the fundamental notion of Thomistic philosophy—"*ens*" ("being")—is a perfect illustration of this term "participation." Thus it is said that "*ens per se*" or "*per essentiam*" is God alone; all other beings "participate" in this perfection, having it in a limited degree, "*per participationem*" from him who possesses it in all its plenitude, namely "*per essentiam.*" St. Thomas applies this same notion to law and explains his meaning quite clearly as we have already shown in our chapter on the Eternal Law. At first glance this application might seem to be limited to human laws

49. "Lex naturalis nihil aliud est quam participatio legis aeternae in rationali creatura" (ibid.).

as they are in the legislator, but a closer reading shows that St. Thomas includes all laws, and consequently the Natural Moral Law, under this concept of "participation" and this notion is in harmony with the active element of the Natural Moral Law, which we will touch on shortly.†

Investigating the meaning of this word as used by St. Thomas in relation to the Natural Moral Law, we find that he used it in a triple sense corresponding to the three elements or angles of the Natural Moral Law which we have just explained.

The first element is expressly mentioned as "participated": "Wherefore it has a share of the Eternal Reason, whereby it has a natural inclination to its proper act and end: and this participation of the eternal law in the rational creature is called the natural law."[50] Further on in the same article we find reference to the second element: "the light of natural reason, whereby we discern what is good and what is evil, which is the function of the natural law, is nothing else than an imprint on us of the divine light. It is therefore evident that the natural law is nothing else than the rational creature's participation of the eternal law."[51]

† **Editor's Note:** For other, recent, considerations of Aquinas's understanding of participation, see Rudi A. te Velde, *Participation and Substantiality in Thomas Aquinas* (Leiden: Brill, 1995); John Rziha, *Perfecting Human Actions: St. Thomas Aquinas on Human Participation in Eternal Law* (Washington, DC: Catholic University of America Press, 2009).

50. "Unde et in ipsa participatur ratio aeterna, per quam habet naturalem inclinationem ad debitum actum et finem. Et talis participatio legis aeternae in rationali creatura lex naturalis dicitur" (ibid.).

51. "Quasi lumen rationis naturalis, quo discernimus quid sit bonum et malum, quod pertinet ad naturalem legem, nihil aliud sit quam impressio divini luminis in nobis. Unde patet quod lex naturalis nihil aliud est quam participatio legis aeternae in rationali creatura" (ibid.). Cf. *De Veritate*, q. 17, a. 3; *In Ps.* 4: 5; *ST* I, q. 88, a. 33, ad 1.

All three elements are brought out even more clearly in a response to an objection: "Even irrational animals partake in their own way of the Eternal Reason, just as the rational creature does [i.e., by natural inclinations]. But because the rational creature partakes thereof in an intellectual [by light of reason] and rational manner [by proposition or actual use of reason], therefore the participation of the eternal law in the rational creature is properly called a law, since a law is something pertaining to reason [proposition of reason]."[52†] Nor is this a strained interpretation of the words of St. Thomas but a distinction given by the Angelic Doctor himself.[53]

This same doctrine is briefly summed up in the *Summa Contra Gentiles*, leaving no room for doubt as to the meaning St. Thomas attached to "participation" in his definition of Natural Moral Law.

> Whatever type of creature carries out the order of divine providence, it is able to do so because it participates in something of the power of the first providential being; just as an instrument does not move unless, through being moved, it participates somewhat in the power of the principal agent. So, the beings that participate more fully in the power of the divine providence are executive agents of divine providence

52. "Etiam animalia irrationalia participant rationem aeternam suo modo, sicut et rationalis creatura [i.e., by natural inclinations]. Sed quia rationalis creatura participat eam intellectualiter [by light of reason] et rationaliter [by proposition or actual use of reason], ideo participatio legis aeternae in creatura rationali proprie lex vocatur, nam lex est aliquid rationis [proposition of reason], ut supra dictum est" (*ST* I-II, q. 91, a. 2, ad 3).

† **Editor's Note:** The bracketed phrases inserted throughout this quotation appear in parentheses in the original text.

53. *II Sent.*, d. 24, q. 3, a. 3, ad 2. Cf. *ST* I, q. 79, a. 8.

in regard to those that participate less. But intellectual creatures participate more than others in it, because an ability to establish order which is done by cognitive power, and an ability to execute it which is done by operative power, are both required for providence, and rational creatures share in both types of power, while the rest of creatures have operative powers only. Therefore, all other creatures are ruled by means of rational creatures under divine providence.[54]

Because our participation in the Eternal Law by reason is the participation par excellence, mention of it is made even outside of the tract on law. For instance: "Now it is from the eternal law, which is the Divine Reason, that human reason is the rule of the human will, from which the human derives its goodness. Hence it is written (Ps. 4): 'Many say: Who showeth us good things? The light of Thy countenance, O Lord, is signed upon us': as though to say: 'The light of our reason is able to show us good things, and guide our will [the precise end of law], insofar as it is the light (i.e., derived from) Thy countenance.'"[55] "Although

54. "Quaecumque creatura exequitur divinae providentiae ordinem, hoc habet inquantum participat aliquid de virtute primi providentis: sicut et instrumentum non movet nisi inquantum per motum participat aliquid de virtute principalis agentis. Quae igitur amplius de virtute divinae providentiae participant, sunt executiva divinae providentiae in illa quae minus participant. Creaturae autem intellectuales plus aliis de ipsa participant: nam, cum ad providentiam requiratur et dispositio ordinis, quae fit per cognoscitivam virtutem, et executio, quae fit per operativam, creaturae rationales utramque virtutem participant, reliquae vero creaturae virtutem operativam tantum. Per creaturas igitur rationales omnes aliae creaturae sub divina providentia reguntur" (*SCG*, lib. III, c. 78).

55. "Quod autem ratio humana sit regula voluntatis humanae, ex qua eius bonitas mensuretur, habet ex lege aeterna, quae est ratio divina. Unde in Psalmo IV, dicitur, multi dicunt, quis ostendit nobis bona? Signatum est super nos lumen

the eternal law is unknown to us according as it is in the Divine Mind: nevertheless, it becomes known to us somewhat, either by natural reason which is derived therefrom as its proper image; or by some sort of additional revelation."[56]

The essence of the Natural Moral Law, therefore, is not an act of reason as Suárez holds, or the result of that act, the proposition, as Sylvius and many modern authors hold. Neither is it in the light of reason as Billuart maintained[57]; nor is it the rational nature itself, the natural inclinations as Vasquez taught.[58] Against each one of these elements taken separately the traditional teaching on the Natural Moral Law presents insuperable difficulties. For instance: how can an act of reason or a proposition of reason be called innate in a sense as strict as the Natural Moral Law is said to be innate, or how can this act or proposition of reason be present in children, or lunatics, as the Natural Moral Law undoubtedly is? How can the light of reason or the natural inclinations be called a law in a sense any higher than we attribute law to the irrational creatures, since moral law even in its subject must have the note of being constituted by reason?

Evidently these three elements must be taken in some way collectively; no less evident is it that they cannot simply be

---

vultus tui, domine, quasi diceret, lumen rationis quod in nobis est, intantum potest nobis ostendere bona, et nostram voluntatem regulare [the precise ends of law], inquantum est lumen vultus tui, idest a vultu tuo derivatum" (*ST* I-II, q. 19, a. 4).

56. "Licet lex aeterna sit nobis ignota secundum quod est in mente divina; innotescit tamen nobis aliqualiter vel per rationem naturalem, quae ab ea derivatur ut propria eius imago; vel per aliqualem revelationem superadditam" (*ST* I-II, q. 19, a. 4, ad 3). Cf. *ST* I, q. 4, a. 1, ad 2 for explanation.

57. *Tract. de Legibus*, Diss. II, a. 2 Dico 2.

58. Vasquez, I-II, d. 150, c. 3 (quoted by Suárez, *De Legibus*, lib. II, c. 5).

bundled together and called the Natural Moral Law, at least if we are to keep to the fundamental doctrine on law exposed by St. Thomas in his general tract on law.[59] The interrelation of these three elements and the part each plays in the Natural Moral Law can be quite readily seen from a consideration of the different texts of St. Thomas where he treats of all three together.

Thus St. Thomas says: "by the natural inclination man is directed to his connatural end. Now the latter happens in respect of two things. First, in respect of the reason or intellect, insofar as it contains the first universal principles which are known to us by the natural light of the intellect, and which are reason's starting-point, both in speculative and in practical matters. Secondly, through the rectitude of the will which tends naturally to good as defined by reason."[60] From this text we see that St. Thomas reduces all three of these elements directly to *nature*; there is no room for freedom here, the three elements flow from the very nature of man and in this sense at least they may be considered of equal value. But is there no definite order between these elements? Is the order given in this text to be taken so strictly?

We have the answer of St. Thomas in two brief texts. "Now in regard to the means, the rectitude of the reason depends on its conformity with the desire of a due end: nevertheless the very desire of the due end presupposes on the part of reason a

59. *ST* I-II, q. 90.

60. "Per naturalem inclinationem ordinatur homo in finem sibi connaturalem. Hoc autem contingit secundum duo. Primo quidem, secundum rationem vel intellectum, inquantum continet prima principia universalia cognita nobis per naturale lumen intellectus, ex quibus procedit ratio tam in speculandis quam in agendis. Secundo, per rectitudinem voluntatis naturaliter tendentis in bonum rationis" (*ST* I-II, q. 62, a. 3).

right apprehension of the end."[61] "The good considered as such, i.e., as appetible, pertains to the will before pertaining to the reason. But considered as true it pertains to the reason, before, under the aspect of goodness, pertaining to the will: because the will cannot desire a good that is not previously apprehended by reason."[62] Here we have the process clearly stated. First is the natural knowledge of the end by virtue of the natural light of reason; then the natural desire for this end on the part of the will; and finally the natural precept of the practical reason flowing from the preceding acts.

This doctrine brings out the dependence of this third element, the proposition of reason, on the other two elements. Indeed it is this very dependence which St. Thomas emphasizes to escape the seemingly vicious circle involved by saying that the rectitude of the practical reason depends on the rectitude of the appetite, and the rectitude of the appetite depends on the practical reason. St. Thomas clears up this difficulty by explaining: "The end and the means pertain to the appetitive faculty, but the end is determined for man by nature... The means are not determined for us by nature but are to be investigated by reason. So it is obvious that rectitude of the appetitive faculty in regard to the end is the measure of truth for the practical reason. According to this the

61. "In his autem quae sunt ad finem, rectitudo rationis consistit in conformitate ad appetitum finis debiti. Sed tamen et ipse appetitus finis debiti praesupponit rectam apprehensionem de fine, quae est per rationem" (*ST* I-II, q. 19, a. 3, ad 2).

62. "Bonum sub ratione boni, idest appetibilis, per prius pertinet ad voluntatem quam ad rationem. Sed tamen per prius pertinet ad rationem sub ratione veri, quam ad voluntatem sub ratione appetibilis, quia appetitus voluntatis non potest esse de bono, nisi prius a ratione apprehendatur" (*ST* I-II, q. 19, a. 3, ad 1).

truth of the practical reason is determined by agreement with a right appetitive faculty. But the truth of the practical reason itself is the rule for the rectitude of the appetitive faculty in regard to the means. According to this, then, the appetitive faculty is called right inasmuch as it pursues the things that reason calls true."[63]

We are now in a position to state the problem of the interrelation of these three elements more fully. The precept of practical reason, i.e., the proposition of reason resulting from this precept, would seem to be the Natural Moral Law in its very essence if we judge it by the principles laid down by St. Thomas as applying to all law. Thus law being the result of a precept which is itself an act of prudence, deals only with the means and not with the end.[64] And it is this third element alone which deals with the means to the end of man. Moreover St. Thomas says unequivocally that law is something constituted by reason[65] and this third element is the only one of the three constituted by reason. This interpretation of the Natural Moral Law as being essentially in the proposition of reason is strengthened by the fact that it is by reason that man is distinguished from other animals, not by his appetite.

On the other hand, this proposition evidently flows from and is immediately dependent upon the natural inclination of man's

63. "Appetitus est finis et eorum quae sunt ad finem: finis autem determinatus est homini a natura, ut supra in III habitum est. Ea autem quae sunt ad finem, non sunt nobis determinata a natura, sed per rationem investigantur; sic ergo manifestum est quod rectitudo appetitus per respectum ad finem est mensura veritatis in ratione practica. Et secundum hoc determinatur veritas rationis practicae secundum concordiam ad appetitum rectum. Ipsa autem veritas rationis practicae est regula rectitudinis appetitus, circa ea quae sunt ad finem. Et ideo secundum hoc dicitur appetitus rectus qui persequitur quae vera ratio dicit" (*VI Ethic.* lect., 2).

64. *ST* II-II, q. 47, a. 8; ibid., q. 50; *ST* I-II, q. 90, a. 4.

65. *ST* I-II, q. 90, a. 1, ad 2; ibid., q. 94, a. 1.

appetite and the natural light of reason; both of which are no less participations of the Eternal Law than the proposition of reason itself. St. Thomas has stated this angle of the Natural Moral Law when he explained that in this law there is an element common to the Natural Laws governing irrational creation and elements peculiar to man[66]; by the natural inclinations this law is brought into relation with the natural physical laws; by the proposition of reason and the light of reason which it presupposes, it is lifted to heights peculiar to man, i.e., to the moral field.

In the *Commentary on the Books of Sentences*, St. Thomas has made an explicit comparison between the natural physical laws and the Natural Moral Law.[67] He explains that creatures enjoying no cognition are directed to their ends directly by their proper forms; creatures enjoying sensitive cognition and appetite are directed to their ends by a natural conception of the cognitive side and a natural inclination to the appetitive side; it is the latter that would seem to be the superior of the natural conception in the matter of directing the creature to its end. But in man, this natural inclination, while still present, cedes its superior position to the natural conception because—the reason is that given by St. Thomas—man knows the end and the proportion of the means to the end. The chief element in the direction of man to his end is not his appetite but his reason, for man directs himself; it is the contrary in the brutes because they do not direct themselves but are driven by another, and it is not their intelligence but another's that is responsible for the direction.

With the superiority of the proposition definitely established as regards the essential nature of Natural Moral Law, there is a

66. *ST* I-II, q. 91, a. 2.

67. *IV Sent.* d. 33, q. 1, a. 1.

temptation to dispose of the natural inclinations by applying the doctrine of St. Thomas regarding precept to this question. Thus the natural inclination takes the place of the act of the election in regard to the ordinary "*imperium*," i.e., the natural inclinations are presupposed in the proposition of reason just as election is presupposed and participated in by the "*imperium*" of the intellect; and, carrying the parallel further, the Natural Moral Law consists essentially in the proposition of reason, just as the "*imperium*" is essentially an act of reason. But the comparison is not so perfect. It is true that the natural inclination of man's appetite gives the motive power to the precept of reason, as does election to the "*imperium*" of reason; but over and above this, this natural inclination "in regard to the end is the measure of truth for the practical reason."[68]

Thus it is clear that the Natural Moral Law is inadequately described unless all three of these elements are taken into consideration. While the precept of natural reason undoubtedly plays the major part, yet it would be unintelligible as a Natural Moral Law without the inclusion of these other two elements which are, as it were, the proximate sources of the proposition of reason.

Taken in this collective sense, this essential notion of law which we have explained answers all these difficulties from the traditional teaching. This will be even more evident when we have finished with our explanation of the Natural Moral Law. Nor does this inclusion of three elements detract from the general principle laid down by St. Thomas concerning law, namely that it must be something constituted by reason[69]; rather it maintains

68. "Per respectum ad finem est mensura veritatis in ratione practica" (*VI Ethic.* lect., 2).

69. *ST* I-II, q. 90, a. 1, ad 2.

this principle and at the same time emphasizes the superiority of the Natural Moral Law in comparison with positive laws.

St. Thomas himself points out some of these elements of superiority. Thus we see clearly how far superior the Natural Moral Law is to human law by the contrast between the feeble impression of a rule of action on the mind of a subject by the precept of a human legislator and the impression by God of His law on the very nature of His subjects, making it an integral part of their being through the natural inclinations and the light of reason and insuring its intelligent observation by means of the natural conception or proposition of reason.[70] The reason for this is given somewhat laconically by St. Thomas when he says: "The natural law is a participation in us of the eternal law: while human law falls short of the eternal law."[71] The one is human, the other divine; the one has the limited effectiveness to be expected from its human authorship; the other penetrates the very being of its subject with all the penetrating intimacy of things divine.

This explanation of the essense of the Natural Moral Law brings out clearly another superiority of the Natural Moral Law over human law—that is the active element of this law in man. Man is not merely a passive subject obeying a law: he participates, in a way, in the active, the legislative side of the law. He plays a dynamic part, or, as St. Thomas puts it, he participates in divine providence in a special way, providing for himself and for others.[72] This gives the Natural Moral Law a completeness that

70. *ST* I-II, q. 93, a. 5; and ibid., ad 1.

71. "Lex naturalis est quaedam participatio legis aeternae in nobis, lex autem humana deficit a lege aeterna" (*ST* I-II, q. 96, a. 2, ad 3).

72. *ST* I-II, q. 91, a. 2; cf. *SCG* III, c. 78.

leaves nothing to be desired and, at the same time, completes the picture of man as participating in the Eternal Law "*per modum imaginis*" ("by way of an image"). For in man, over and above the natural inclinations by which he passively participates in the Eternal Law in common with irrational creatures, and the light of reason by which he passively participates in it in a manner proper to himself, there is an active participation in this law by the act of reason and the proposition constituted by this act by which man provides both for himself and for others.

There is one difficulty to be cleared up in regard to this explanation of the essence of the Natural Moral Law, namely, the determination of the exact nature of this third element, the proposition of reason. We shall treat of this immediately in explaining the precepts of the Natural Moral Law.

* * *

# Chapter V

# Connected Problems: Criticism of Suárez

## I. Precepts of the Natural Moral Law

We can best understand this third element of the Natural Moral Law—the proposition of reason—by considering it in its origin. The first thing a man knows in the speculative order, i.e., the purely intellectual order without any proximate ordination to action, is "being"—"*ens*." The reason for this is that this notion is included in everything that man apprehends; nothingness is incomprehensible. Thus the first principle of the speculative order is that founded on the notion of being, namely the principles of identity and contradiction.[1]

Coming down from the speculative order to the order of action, the practical order, we see that the first thing apprehended by the practical reason is the notion of good.[†] The practical reason ordains its knowledge to a definite work or operation; that is, it understands, not merely for the sake of understanding, but to apply this knowledge to operation. In this work or operation, man always aims at some end; and this end in itself includes the notion of the good—"*bonum.*" The parallel is quite perfect: just as in the speculative intellect everything apprehended includes the notion of being, which is the principle of comprehension. So in the practical order, everything apprehended includes the notion of the good, for it is the good, constituted as end, which draws men to actual operation and which is consequently the first mover of the practical order, the first principle is that founded on the notion of good. The basic notion of good is its desirability; it might be stated as: "Good is what all desire." The principle founded on this notion is: "Good is to be done, evil is to be avoided."

**1. First Precepts.** This principle St. Thomas calls the first precept of the Natural Moral Law.[2] It is the third of the essential elements of the Natural Moral Law which we have explained

1. *ST* I-II, q. 94, a. 2.

† **Editor's Note:** The distinction between and the integration of the speculative and the practical orders is very important. The end of speculative knowledge is the truth for truth's sake. The end of practical knowledge is the truth for the sake of some further operation (under the aspect of good, of course). Aquinas explains: "Now, to a thing apprehended by the intellect, it is accidental whether it be directed to operation or not, and according to this the speculative and practical intellects differ. For it is the speculative intellect which directs what it apprehends, not to operation, but solely to the consideration of truth; while the practical intellect is that which directs what it apprehends to operation" (*ST* I, q. 79, a. 11). However, the "aspect of truth" remains even in practical reason's the further ordination to action: "The object of the practical intellect is good directed to operation, and under the aspect of truth. For the practical intellect knows truth, just as the speculative, but it directs the known truth to operation" (*ST* I, q. 79, a. 11, ad 2). There can be speculative knowledge without any further practical use of knowledge. But there cannot be any practical knowledge without some prior and fundamental practical knowledge. Otherwise put, we cannot put our knowledge of something into action unless we first have some knowledge of what this something is. Truth exercises a shaping influence in the speculative and practical orders both. Cf. *De Veritate*, q. 2, a. 8.

2. Ibid.

above for it includes all other precepts. Moreover it is naturally known, that is, it is a first principle, known as soon as its terms are understood, in this case, from the dawn of reason. This is apparent if we thoroughly understand the principle. The purpose of the inclinations of man are to direct him to his end, since they are a part of the Natural Moral Law; as this end, like all ends, includes the notion of good, everything to which the natural inclinations of man incline him will be judged to be good by the practical intellect and consequently to be done. The things contrary to these inclinations, since they will lead a man away from his end and consequently from the good, will be apprehended, naturally, as bad and to be avoided. It is to be particularly noted that this apprehension is natural, i.e., it is not free: the principle is known of itself, just as the first principle of the speculative order is known immediately without reasoning or investigation.[3] It is a part of that participation in the Eternal Law which is the Natural Moral Law. It comes as naturally to a man as do his natural inclinations and the natural light of reason, but is nonetheless, eminently reasonable.

**2. Classification of the Precepts.**

(A) According to the order of origin. Since the foundation of the notion of good and bad apprehended by the practical intellect is the convenience or inconvenience to the natural inclinations, it follows that we can classify these precepts (which are commands to do the convenient and avoid the inconvenient) according to the classification of the inclinations themselves. This classification is triplex[4]:

3. Ibid.
4. Ibid.; ibid., ad 2; ibid., ad 3; ibid., a. 4, ad 3.

1. Those precepts which proceed from the natural inclinations which man has in common with all substances, namely the inclination to conserve his existence. Such precepts are those pertaining to the conservation of human life.
2. Those precepts which proceed from the natural inclinations man has in common with other animals. Such precepts are those commanding the generation and education of children, etc.
3. Those precepts which proceed from the natural inclinations which are proper to man himself, i.e., as a rational creature. Such are: that he avoid ignorance (in accordance with his natural inclination to know truth); that he must not offend others with whom he should live (according to his inclination to live in society), etc.[†]

This division is evident. But it must be noted that those precepts of the first and second class, inasmuch as they are human acts and hence subject to Natural Moral Law, are no less rational than those of the third class. Though man's nature is virtually vegetative and sensitive, it is formally rational and this rational

† **Editor's Note:** It is important to note that Aquinas does not cite a generic inclination to the good of truth in *ST* I-II, q. 94, a. 2. Rather, he identifies a specific "natural inclination to know the truth about God" ("*homo habet naturalem inclinationem ad hoc quod veritatem cognoscat de Deo*"). This point is often overlooked in contemporary natural law discussions. For Aquinas, the natural law has a "theonomic" origin and constitution. He does not conceive of a robust natural law doctrine separated from a natural knowledge of God (and man's orientation thereto). God stands at the center of any authentically Thomistic natural law doctrine. For more on this, see Cajetan Cuddy, O.P., "Thomas Aquinas on the Bible and Morality: The Sacred Scriptures, the Natural Law, and the Hermeneutic of Continuity," in *Towards a Biblical Thomism: Thomas Aquinas and the Renewal of Biblical Theology*, ed. Jörgen Vijgen and Piotr Roszak (Pamplona: EUNSA, 2018), pp. 173–97.

form extends its empire to all of man's deliberate actions, even though they proceed directly from other potencies.[5]

(B) According to the cognoscibility of the precepts. This second classification might also be called the order of proximity to nature, or the order of defectibility or indefectibility. But as all these points will be brought out as our treatment of the precepts proceeds the present title will be comprehensive enough. This classification is also triplex:

1. *Primary Precepts*—those which are indemonstrable principles, "*per se nota*," like those of the speculative order. These flow from nature itself, are taught by nature and need no other promulgation.[6] Such are, for instance, "good is to be done, evil is to be avoided."[7]
2. *Secondary Precepts*—which are immediate conclusions from the primary precepts[8]; are seen with very little consideration by even the unlearned[9]; flow from nature itself through the primary precepts and reason[10] and thus pertain directly to the Natural Moral Law. Such precepts are the Ten Commandments.[11]
3. *Remote Conclusions*—from these first and secondary precepts. They demand long consideration and can be discovered by

5. *ST* I-II, q. 94, a. 2; ibid., a. 4; ibid., a. 6; *ST* I-II, q. 100, a. 11.
6. *ST* I-II, q. 100, a. 3; ibid., a. 11.
7. "Bonum est faciendum, malum vitandum" (*ST* I-II, q. 94, a. 2).
8. *ST* I-II, q. 94, a. 4, *corp.* and ad 2; ibid., a. 5; *ST* I-II, q. 100, a. 11. Mentioned also in *ST* I-II, q. 94, a. 6, *corp.*, and ad 1 and ad 3; *ST* I-II, q. 97, a. 4, ad 3.
9. *ST* I-II, q. 100, a. 1; ibid., a. 3; ibid., a. 11.
10. *ST* I-II, q. 100, a. 11, ad 2.
11. *ST* I-II, q. 100, a. 3 and a. 11.

> the wise only.[12] The reason being that in contingent things, in which fall human operations, the closer one descends to proper or particular things, the greater are the probabilities of defect and error.[13]

This same triplex division is to be found in the other works of St. Thomas with the same explanation of each division.[14] But it is to be noted that in the tract on the Natural Moral Law itself, St. Thomas mentions only the primary and secondary precepts. The reason for this is quite evident. The primary precepts are a part of the essence of the Natural Moral Law itself, making up the third element—the proposition of reason; the secondary precepts are so intimately connected with these primary precepts, are seen by everyone with no help other than that of nature itself, that they are intimately a part of the law. The remote conclusions are not so intimately bound up with the very essence of the law, since their discovery is limited to the learned and they demand such long thought over and above the teachings of nature itself.

The reason for classification is nicely stated by St. Thomas when he explains that law is the art of ordaining human life; like all arts it should have a distinction of rules or precepts, otherwise the confusion of precepts will destroy the utility of the laws.[15] This general reason is supplemented by a profound explanation of this triplex classification which we will treat under the heading

12. *ST* I-II, q. 100, a. 1; ibid., a. 3; ibid., a. 11.

13. *ST* I-II, q. 94, a. 4.

14. E.g., *V Ethic.* lect. 12; *III Sent.* d. 37, q. 1, a. 3; *IV Sent.* d. 33, q. 1, a. 1 (explains only primary and secondary precepts).

15. *ST* I-II, q. 104, a. 4.

of "the scope of the precepts of the Natural Moral Law." But first it will be necessary to explain the distinction of law and precept.

**3. Distinction of Law and Precept.** The origin of this difficulty in speaking of law in general is evident from our treatment of law in our first chapter, where we showed that St. Thomas evidently defined law as a precept and also that there is a great deal of variety of opinion among the authors as to just what distinction should be placed between law and precept. From our explanation of the essential nature of the Natural Moral Law, this difference in regard to the Natural Moral Law is immediately apparent since the precept or proposition of reason is, at most, but one of three essential elements of the law. Taking the active element of the Natural Moral Law alone, the proposition of reason, we see that St. Thomas identifies it, at least as regards the primary precepts, with the precepts; and this is in accordance with his general doctrine on law, taken as it is in the subject.

He defines law as a common precept.[16] Yet he says that precept implies the application of the law to the things regulated by the law,[17] thus apparently contradicting himself. A more attentive reading shows that this is not a contradiction but a full expression of the thought of St. Thomas on precepts. It will be noted that he does not say that precept is the application of the law, as does Cajetan,[18] but that it *implies* this application.[19] His real thought is that the precepts can be considered from a double point of view: either from the standpoint of their common order to the same

16. *ST* I-II, q. 98, a. 6, ad 2; ibid., q. 90, a. 1 and 2; ibid., q. 92, a. 2, ad 1.
17. *ST* I-II, q. 90, a. 2, ad 1.
18. Cajetan in I-II, q. 90, a. 2, ad 1.
19. *ST* I-II, q. 90, a. 2, ad 1.

end; or from the standpoint of the particular things to which they imply an application. In the first sense, the common or universal precepts coalesce into one and coincide with positive law as it is in the subject, and, in the case of Natural Moral Law, with the active element of the Natural Moral Law—the proposition of reason. In the second sense, they are multiple and can be said to be distinct from the law.[20]

It is evident that St. Thomas thus uses the word precept in a sense much wider than we give the word today; indeed he says as much expressly.[21] It is also evident from the whole context of his tract on law, for example he says quite plainly, speaking of the most general, or primary precepts of the Natural Moral Law, that they are really the ends of the precepts, i.e., taking precepts in the narrower sense in which we use the word today.[22]

**4. Scope of the Precepts.** In a wide and improper sense, all virtues may be said to fall under the Natural Moral Law. That is, if we consider them, not precisely as virtues, but as acts of reason and consequently according to reason. The explanation of this is quite simple. Those things to which man has a natural inclination are said to pertain to the Natural Moral Law; man has a natural inclination to act according to reason since every being has the inclination to act according to its form and the rational soul is the form of man.[23] In this sense all sins are against nature because all sins are against reason.[24]

---

20. *ST* I-II, q. 99, a. 1; ibid., ad 1; *ST* I-II, q. 94, a. 2, ad 1.
21. *ST* I-II, q. 92, a. 2, ad 1.
22. *ST* I-II, q. 100, a. 11.
23. *ST* I-II, q. 94, a. 3.
24. Ibid., ad 2.

Considering virtues according to their proper species, that is precisely as virtues, and not from the general aspect of acts of reason, the scope of the precepts of the Natural Moral Law is much more limited, since "much is done according to virtue to which nature does not immediately incline a man."[25]

Properly speaking, the scope of the precepts of the Natural Moral Law is really a corollary from the doctrine of the essence of this law and the nature of the precepts. The purpose of the inclinations (a part of the essence of the law) is to lead man to his end. Hence what is opposed to these inclinations, and consequently to reason, will be opposed to his attaining his end. Since this end has the "*ratio boni*" ("nature" or "character of goodness") these things opposed to the attainment of the end will have, in themselves, the "*ratio mali*" ("nature" or "character of evil") i.e., they will be "*in se mala*" ("evil in themselves").[26] This is the meaning of St. Thomas when he lays down the general rule: "a thing is so much the more easily grasped by the reason, as its contrary is more grievous and repugnant to reason."[27]

This opposition to the attainment of the end can be of three kinds or degrees: (a) such as will altogether prohibit the attainment of the principal end of man; (b) such as will make its attainment less congruous, less becoming; (c) such as will make impossible the attainment, not of the primary end of man, but of a secondary end.[28] It will be noted at once that these "*in se mala*," or things opposed to the end of man, fall into a division

25. *ST* I-II, q. 94, a. 3.

26. *IV Sent.* d. 15, q. 3, a. 1, sol. 4.

27. "Tanto aliquid magis a ratione suscipitur, quanto contrarium est gravius et magis rationi repugnans" (*ST* I-II, q. 100, a. 6).

28. *IV Sent.* d. 33, q. 1, a. 1.

corresponding to the order of precepts according to their cognoscibility. It is these "*in se mala*" and their opposites, "*in se bona*," which are the proper matter of the precepts of the Natural Moral Law.[29]

The correctness of this limitation of the scope of the precepts of the Natural Moral Law to "*in se bona*" and "*in se mala*" receives a confirmation from a momentary consideration of the intention of the legislator in framing the law and of the ordinary course followed in nature. From the first point of view, it is evident that the intention of the legislator was to lead men to virtue; hence in assigning the precepts, he used the "way of virtue," i.e., proceeding "from those things which are easier [more manifest] to the more difficult," as is also the method employed in purely speculative cognition.[30] It was necessary to start from the very elementals; and it is with these elementals that the Natural Moral Law deals: "The precepts of the natural law are general, and require to be determined: and they are determined both by human law and by Divine law. And just as these very determinations which are made by human law are said to be, not of natural, but of positive law; so the determinations of the precepts of the natural law, effected by the Divine law, are distinct from the moral precepts which belong to the natural law."[31] It was not necessary to command all acts

29. *IV Sent.* d. 15, q. 3, a. 1, sol. 4; *ST* I-II, q. 100, a. 1; *II Sent.* d. 42, q. 2, a. 5.

30. "Ex his quae magis in promptu sunt, in difficiliora tendatur" (*III Sent.* d. 37, q. 1, a. 2, sol. 1).

31. "Praecepta legis naturae communia sunt, et indigent determinatione. Determinantur autem et per legem humanam, et per legem divinam. Et sicut ipsae determinationes quae fiunt per legem humanam, non dicuntur esse de lege naturae, sed de iure positivo; ita ipsae determinationes praeceptorum legis naturae quae fiunt per legem divinam, distinguuntur a praeceptis moralibus, quae pertinent ad legem naturae" (*ST* I-II, q. 99, a. 3, ad 2). Cf. ibid., a. 4.

of virtue—this would be perfection; but only those "*quae primo occurrunt facienda*," i.e., those things without which the order of reason (the order to an end) could not be observed.[32]

Looking at the order observed in the workings of the things of nature we have another confirmation of this limitation of the Natural Law to the very fundamentals. "As nature proceeds from small seeds to giant trees, so also law proceeds from those things that are in the beginning and just starting [*in promptu*] to other things which are sometimes more difficult and more perfect."[33]

**5. Stability of the Precepts.** In treating of the stability of the Natural Moral Law, we limit ourselves to the precepts because it is self-evident that the natural inclinations and the light of reason are absolutely immutable and universal, being an intimate part of human nature.[34] Nor is there any difficulty about a change in the law by way of addition; since the law remains intact after such a change as before it,[35] the only difficulty arises from a change in the law by way of subtraction—i.e., something that was formerly a part of the law, ceases to be so. Considering the precepts in order we find:

1. *Primary precepts*—are the same everywhere and are equally known by all.[36] They are absolutely immutable[37] and hence

32. *III Sent.* d. 37, q. 1, a. 2, sol. 1.
33. "Sicut enim natura ex parvis seminibus in maximas arbores proficit, ita etiam et lex ex his quae in principio et in promptu sunt, in alia procedit, quae sunt quandoque difficiliora et perfectiora" (ibid., ad 2).
34. *De Veritate*, q. 16, a. 3, *corp.* and ad 5.
35. *ST* I-II, q. 94, a. 5.
36. *ST* I-II, q. 94, a. 4; *V Ethic.* lect. 12.
37. *ST* I-II, q. 94, a. 5; *III Sent.* d. 37, q. 1, a. 3; *IV Sent.* d. 33, q. 1, a. 1.

can never be erased from the heart of man.[38] St. Thomas shows that the particular application of these universal principles may be erased from the heart of man in several ways, for instance through a lack of attention, or on account of some impediment, such as corporal infirmity or through passion.[39] But this is really the work of conscience and has no direct relation to the present question.

2. *Secondary Precepts*—are the same everywhere, "*ut in pluribus*," both as regards the precepts in themselves ("*quantum ad rectitudinem*") and as regards their recognition by men.[40] That is to say, they are morally universal, to be found in the very great majority of men. St. Thomas warns us that we are dealing here with human things and must not expect a metaphysical certitude: "'We must not seek the same degree of certainty in all things' (*I Ethic.* lect. 3). Consequently in contingent matters, such as natural and human things, it is enough for a thing to be certain, as being true in the greater number of instances, though at times and less frequently it fail."[41] By way of exception, "*ut in paucioribus*," these secondary precepts may be changed:
   (a) *Quantum ad rectitudinem*—i.e., as regards the binding force of the precepts considered in themselves, on account of some particular

38. *ST* I-II, q. 94, a. 6.
39. *ST* I-II, q. 99, a. 2, ad 2; ibid., q. 77, a. 2. Cf. *De Veritate*, q. 16, a. 3 and q. 17, a. 2; *II Sent.* d. 24, q. 3, a. 3, *corp.* and objections.
40. *ST* I-II, q. 94, a. 4.
41. "Non est eadem certitudo quaerenda in omnibus, ut in *I Ethic.* dicitur. Unde in rebus contingentibus, sicut sunt naturalia et res humanae, sufficit talis certitudo ut aliquid sit verum ut in pluribus, licet interdum deficiat in paucioribus" (*ST* I-II, q. 96, a. 1, ad 3).

impediments.[42] A closer reading of this text, and a comparison with parallel passages in the commentary on the *Books of Ethics*[43] and the *Third Book of Sentences*,[44] makes it evident that St. Thomas means that circumstances may change the particular material which otherwise would fall under these precepts, but which because of these new circumstances, is no longer the proper material of these precepts. This is particularly evident from the example St. Thomas repeats again and again,[45] namely: a deposit should be returned to the depositor, but in the case, for instance, that it was a weapon which was deposited, and at the present moment the depositor calling for his property is in such a state of mind (through anger or insanity, for example) that he would certainly do some harm were the weapon given to him. Evidently the precept of justice, commanding that his property be returned to him, does not bind. It is also evident that this is really a change in the material and not a change in the precept, as a full statement of the precept would make clear.

(b) *Quantum ad notitiam*—that is, as regards the knowledge men have of these precepts.[46] For this failure of the Natural Moral Law, St. Thomas

42. *ST* I-II, q. 94, a. 4.
43. *V Ethic.* lect. 12.
44. *III Sent.* d. 37, q. 1, a. 3.
45. E.g., *III Sent.* d. 37, q. 1, a. 3.
46. *ST* I-II, q. 94, a. 4; ibid., q. 99, a. 2, ad 2.

assigns three causes[47]: depraved reason, thus a man is not able to draw these evident conclusions from the primary precepts; evil customs which, preceding the proper use of reason or stifling, hide the evidence of these conclusions; corrupt habits, or as St. Thomas calls it in another place,[48] "*defectus amor boni*," i.e., a perversion of the appetitive faculties.

3. *Remote Conclusions*—the general rule concerning these conclusions can be found briefly stated in this tract on Natural Moral Law, though St. Thomas does not treat of them explicitly in this place. He says: "Although there is necessity in the general principles [of practical reason], the more we descend to matters of detail, the more frequently we encounter defects."[49] Their variability is easily seen when we consider that their recognition demands a long consideration of diverse circumstances and is limited to the wise.[50] Thus we see at once three very potent sources of variety and of error: (a) the lengthy consideration involved giving room for the variety and admixture of error that follows on the lengthy intellectual labors of individual men; (b) the variety of circumstances, different in almost every case; (c) the actual intellectual capacity of the man drawing these conclusions. It is then evident that these remote conclusions are not everywhere the same, nor are they equally known by all

47. *ST* I-II, q. 94, a. 4. Cf. ibid., a. 6.

48. *III Sent.* d. 37, q. 1, a. 1. Cf. *ST* I-II, q. 94, a. 6.

49. "Etsi in communibus [ratio practica] sit aliqua necessitas, quanto magis ad propria descenditur, tanto magis invenitur defectus" (*ST* I-II, q. 94, a. 4).

50. *ST* I-II, q. 100, a. 1.

> men; and they can very easily be erased from the minds of men by any of the causes assigned for the corruption of the secondary precepts as regards their recognition, as well as by the three causes assigned for the variety of these remote conclusions themselves.

The stability and variability of the precepts of the Natural Moral Law will be seen more clearly if we glance for a moment at their causes. The primary precepts, as we have already explained, are a part of the essence of the Natural Moral Law, as immutable as the natural inclinations and the light of reason in man. As in the inclinations and the light of reason, liberty has no part to play, there is no chance for human error, for these primary precepts are evident in themselves, forcing the assent of the intellect. Because of this, some have traced the immutability of the Natural Moral Law to the immutability of the essentials of human nature; and this is true if rightly understood. But St. Thomas would leave no room for misunderstanding, seeking out the source of this immutability and stating it plainly: "The natural and Divine laws proceed from the Divine will.... Wherefore they cannot be changed by a custom proceeding from the will of man."[51] The real root of this immutability is the Eternal Law; these primary precepts are a part of the impression of that law on man.

Because of the intimate connection between the primary and secondary precepts, St. Thomas admits no real objective change

51. "Lex naturalis et divina procedit a voluntate divina.... Unde non potest mutari per consuetudinem procedentem a voluntate hominis" (*ST* I-II, q. 97, a. 3, ad 1).

in the secondary precepts. The change he does admit, as regards their recognition by men, and the variability of the remote conclusions is due to the entrance of the human factor—what St. Thomas frequently calls the "mutability of human nature." Among such human factors he mentions diverse conditions and states of men, diverse conditions of persons, times, and other circumstances, etc.[52]

**6. Dispensation from the Precepts.** All theologians are agreed on the question we have just treated, namely that there can be no intrinsic change in the precepts of the Natural Moral Law. The dispute about the mutability of these precepts is in reference to the external mutability of this law or the possibility of dispensation from it. There is no question about the primary precepts of the Natural Moral Law, all theologians being agreed that there can be no dispensation from these precepts; the question centers about the possibility of a dispensation from the secondary precepts, i.e., from the Ten Commandments. And even here, the question is strictly limited to divine authority granting the dispensation.

To understand this question thoroughly it is necessary to distinguish the two kinds of dispensation: dispensation properly and improperly so-called. Dispensation, properly taken, is defined as: "A relaxation of the law or of its obligations in a particular instance by someone having power, with the matter of the law remaining unchanged, so that its obligation would remain if the authority had not given a dispensation." Improper dispensation is

52. Cf. *ST* II-II, q. 57, a. 2, ad 1; *Supplem.* q. 41, a. 1, ad 3; ibid., a. 2 and a. 4; ibid., q. 65, a. 2, *corp.* and ad 1; *De Malo* q. 2, a. 4, ad 13; *ST* I-II, q. 94, a. 3, ad 3; ibid., q. 66, a. 1.

had: "when a legislator or someone else so changes the matter of the law that it ceases to be under the law."[53]

The question to be solved is: whether God, by His absolute power, can dispense from the Ten Commandments.

St. Thomas answers without any qualification that the precepts of the Decalogue are altogether indispensable.[54] The foundation of this position of St. Thomas is readily seen from our exposition of law in general and the Natural Moral Law in particular. These precepts do not depend on the will of God; they are not extrinsically but intrinsically valid, for the Natural Moral Law, like all law, is essentially the work of reason, not of will; in this case it is the divine reason which cannot be changed. Billuart offers further proof of this position by pointing out that God cannot dispense from a necessary law, and the Natural Moral Law is necessary supposing the will of God to create man; that the precepts of the Natural Moral Law are founded in the nature of man; and that the Natural Moral Law is really a part of the Eternal Law if we take the former law objectively, while subjectively it is a participation of the Eternal Law—all of which are very solid arguments against the possibility of dispensation.[55] But the fundamental and adequate reason against dispensation is that which is drawn from the intrinsic nature of this law as a work of divine reason.

---

53. "Relaxatio legis seu ejus obligationis in aliquo particulari facta ab habente potestatem, manente materia legis sic immutata ut ejus obligatio remaneret si non accederet auctoritas dispensanti.... Quando Legislator vel alter sic mutat materiam legis, ut desinat comprehendi sub legi" (Billuart, *Tract. de Legibus*, Diss. II, a. 4).

54. *ST* I-II, q. 100, a. 8.

55. Billuart, *Tract. de Legibus*, Diss. II, a. 4.

St. Thomas sums up his position when he says: "God cannot dispense a man so that it be lawful for him not to direct himself to God, or not to be subject to His justice, even in those matters in which men are directed to one another."[56] This is precisely and exclusively the work of the Natural Moral Law—to ordain man to his end; its precepts touch only those things that of themselves lead man to this end or of themselves lead man away from this end. The distinction placed on these words of St. Thomas by Scotists—that if there were a divine dispensation from these precepts their violation would no longer be an ordination—rests on the assumption that the Natural Moral Law and the consequent moral goodness and malice of human acts governed by it are extrinsic things. We have already treated of this point of view in exposing St. Thomas's notion of the essence of the Natural Moral Law; the fallacy of this position will be more apparent from a discussion of the obligation of the Natural Moral Law and from our criticism of Suárez.

Suárez is in complete agreement with this doctrine of St. Thomas on dispensation from the Natural Moral Law.[57] Nor is he illogical in this position, in spite of his holding, with Scotus,[58] that the Natural Moral Law depends essentially on the will and not on the reason of God, and is thus extrinsic. The morality caused by the Natural Moral Law is indeed distinct from the "natural honesty and malice" of acts, according to Suárez, yet *de*

56. "Et ideo in hoc Deus dispensare non potest, ut homini liceat non ordinate se habere ad Deum, vel non subdi ordini iustitiae eius, etiam in his secundum quae homines ad invicem ordinantur" (*ST* I-II, q. 100, a. 8, ad 2). Cf. ibid., q. 104, a. 1.

57. Suárez, *De Legibus*, lib. II, c. 15.

58. Scotus, *IV Sent.*; lib. I, d. 44, 2.

*facto* these two moralities are inseparable and God cannot refrain from commanding and prohibiting the acts which form the subject matter of the Natural Moral Law.[59]

Against this position of the absolute indispensability of the Natural Moral Law is the opinion of Scotus. According to Scotus,[60] precepts can be said to pertain to the Natural Moral Law in two ways: strictly speaking and taking the word in a larger sense. Those precepts pertain to the Natural Moral Law in the first way which are necessary practical principles, known as soon as their terms are known, or necessary conclusions from these principles. Such are the first two precepts of the Decalogue. Speaking less strictly, a precept is said to pertain to the Natural Moral Law, not because it follows necessarily from the principles of that law, but because it is very much in harmony with that law ("*multum consona illi legi*").

According to Frassen, a trustworthy commentator of Scotus, both of these classes of precepts are strictly a part of the Natural Law. The second class, or those merely in harmony with the principles of the Natural Moral Law, are properly and strictly a part of natural law and they oblige independently of the act of any will commanding or prohibiting; the others, the first two precepts of the Decalogue, are most strictly a part of the Natural Moral Law, so strict that they admit of no dispensation even by the absolute power of God.[61] But from his explanations given in other places[62] it is evident that by "any will" Frassen here means positive law,

59. Suárez, *De Legibus*, lib. II, c. 15, no. 4.

60. Scotus, *III Sent.*, d. 37, q. unica, 5ff.; and in *IV Sent.*, d. 17, q. 1, 3.

61. Claude Frassen, *Scotus Academicus* (Rome: Ex Typographia Sallustiana, 1901), VI: p. 67.

62. E.g., ibid., p. 75, p. 90.

being quite willing to concede a dependence of these precepts on the will of God, which is indeed the basis of dispensation. He may be stretching the meaning of Scotus a bit in making all the precepts of the Decalogue pertain strictly to the Natural Moral Law, for Scotus himself used such expressions as "very much in harmony with the law,"[63] "to be of the natural law.... broadly speaking,"[64] and "strictly speaking, nothing is of the law of nature except the demonstrated principle or conclusion; yet sometimes something is said to be of the law of nature in an extended sense,"[65] as descriptive of these last seven precepts of the Decalogue.

Scotus places still another distinction in the precepts, pointing out that every precept has a double element: negative and positive. When a precept is simply negative, then the affirmative precept implied in it only determines the mean conducive to the observance of this negative precept; when the precept is simply affirmative, then the negative precept involved in it determines only the medium necessary for the observance of the affirmative precept.[66]

These distinctions being placed, we are in a position to state Scotus's theory, which is: God, by His absolute power, can dispense, in the strict sense of the word, from the precepts of the Decalogue which do not refer directly to God, with the exception of the precept against lying[67] and perhaps the precept referring

63. "Multum consona illi legi" (Scotus, *III Sent.*, d. 37, q. unica).

64. "Esse de lege naturae.... large loquendo" (ibid).

65. "Stricte loquendo, nihil aliud est de lege naturae, nisi principium vel conclusio demonstrata; sic tamen extendendo quandoque illud dicitur esse de lege naturae" (Scotus, *IV Sent.*, d. 17, 19).

66. Scotus, *III Sent.*, d. 37, 7; Frassen, *Scotus Academicus*, p. 84.

67. Scotus, *III Sent.*, d. 37, 5; Frassen, *Scotus Academicus*, p. 84.

to the worship of God, taking this precept as regards its affirmative element[68]; God cannot dispense, even by His absolute power, from the first two precepts of the Decalogue and from the third taken negatively.

For purposes of criticism we need only take the first part of this thesis, for it is here precisely that the question centers. This opinion of Scotus rests on whether or not these precepts of the Decalogue which do not refer to God, i.e., the last seven, pertain to the Natural Moral Law as necessary conclusions from the principles of the law. Our whole exposition of the precepts of the Natural Moral Law according to St. Thomas was a proof that they are such necessary conclusions; consequently Scotus's arguments will rather be of a negative character, tending to disprove this argument of St. Thomas. Scotus offers three arguments to prove his position, which are admirably summed up and criticized by Cajetan.[69] We are following the criticism of Cajetan.

*First Argument*[70]: These precepts do not pertain to the Natural Moral Law as necessary principles or as necessary conclusions from the principles of the Natural Moral Law. This is easily seen, because if they did, they would be altogether indispensable, whereas *de facto* God granted dispensations from them, e.g., the command to Abraham to kill his son. That these precepts would be indispensable follows from the fact that such necessary conclusions are true in themselves before a relation exists to an intellect; the divine will could not be good or right ("*recta*") in willing their opposites, so consequently it could not dispense.

68. Scotus, *III Sent.*, d. 37, 6; Frassen, *Scotus Academicus*, pp. 91ff.

69. Cajetan in I-II, q. 100, a. 8.

70. Scotus, *III Sent.*, d. 37, 4.

*Criticism*: The fact alleged is not an example of true dispensation, as can be seen by the explanations in all the authors.[71] As to the reason brought forth to prove that these precepts would be altogether indispensable if they were necessary conclusions from the principles of the Natural Moral Law, it is quite true and is indeed the position of the Thomists. It has no demonstrating effect here because the will of God did not will the opposites in the examples given from the Old Testament. We have not gone into this *de facto* argument, first because it is necessarily too long for the place of Scotus in this dissertation; secondly, because exhaustive interpretations of these facts can be found in the sources we have indicated. We prefer rather to deal with the fundamental reasons behind the theory of Scotus.

*Second Argument*[72]: If these precepts of the Decalogue do not pertain to the Natural Moral Law as simply being in harmony with the principles of that law, but rather are necessary conclusions from those principles dealing with things necessarily good and necessarily bad, then the divine will is necessarily and simply determined to things other than itself just as the intellect is determined to understand the necessarily true.

*Criticism*: This determination can be understood in two ways: (a) as meaning that the divine will would be determined to will the existence of these things; (b) meaning that the divine will would be determined as regards the goodness and malice of these things. The first sense is false, for all being is the result of a free act of God. The second sense carries with it no inconvenience, as is

71. E.g., St. Thomas, I-II, q. 100, a. 8, ad 3; Cajetan in I-II, q. 100, a. 8, no. 2; Suárez, *De Legibus*, lib. II, c. 15, no. 20; Billuart, *Tract. de Legibus*, Diss. II, a. 4, ad 1.

72. Scotus, *III Sent.*, d. 37, 4.

evident from the fact that there are precepts, admitted by Scotus himself, dealing with things necessarily good and necessarily bad, e.g., the first two precepts of the Decalogue. The sense of this determination is that the divine will cannot refuse to be in accord with the right and cannot be in accord with the wrong. Cajetan expresses this determination in God very well when he says: "as the Divine Intellect is naturally determined only to understanding God Himself and all that naturally shines forth in Him; so the Divine Will [is naturally determined] to willing God Himself, and all that is naturally right; things of this sort, only exist in God, before they are communicated by Him."[73]

*Third Argument*[74]: In the things commanded or prohibited by these precepts under discussion, there is not a goodness necessary to the goodness of the final end, or necessarily leading to the ultimate end; in the evils prohibited there is not a malice necessarily turning man away from the final end. If this good were not commanded the final end could still be attained and loved; if the evil were not prohibited, the attainment of the final end would still be possible. Consequently these precepts cannot be necessary conclusions from the principles of the Natural Moral Law.

*Criticism*: This argument has a triple sense. (a) In these precepts there is not a goodness that has a necessary connection with the final end. In this sense the argument is false. The proof adduced in favor of it does not prove a contingent connection

73. "Sicut divinus intellectus naturaliter determinatus est ad Deum ipsum tantum intelligendum, et in se omnia naturaliter relucentia; ita divina voluntas ad Deum ipsum tantum volendum, et in seipsa omnia naturaliter recta, qualia sunt huiusmodi, quae non nisi in Deo sunt, antequam ab ipso communicarentur" (Cajetan in I-II, q. 100, a. 8, no. 3).

74. Scotus, *III Sent.*, d. 37, 5; Frassen, *Scotus Academicus*, p. 94.

but merely shows that the end does not depend from the conclusions necessarily inferred from it; just as from the fact that the principles are true without the conclusions it does not follow that the conclusions are not necessarily connected with the end or are not necessary in themselves, but only that the truth and knowledge of the principles do not depend upon the conclusions. (b) In these precepts there is not a goodness necessary to the existence and love of the final end. In this sense the assumption is true. But from this it does not follow that the conclusions are not necessary. (c) In these precepts there is not a goodness necessarily leading to the final end, nor an evil necessarily averting from that end. In this sense the assumption is false. Just as in necessary conclusions there is a truth leading *a posteriori* to the first principles, so here there is a goodness in the conclusions leading necessarily *a posteriori* to the final end. The proof is a sophism which Cajetan calls the "sophism of the consequent,"[75] i.e., if it is true it proves only that the conversion or aversion in regard to the final end does not depend solely on these things, but can be had also from other sources; these conclusions lead to or avert from the end *a posteriori*. Yet as Cajetan says, these things commanded by the latter precepts of the Decalogue are so necessarily connected with the final end that conversion to these goods and aversion from these evils, at least in "*praeparatione animae*" ("the preparedness of the soul") is inseparable from the love of the final end.

So much for the arguments of Scotus. For a decisive refutation of his theory it is necessary to seek its foundation. Evidently Scotus agrees that the necessary principles of the Natural Moral

75. Cajetan in I-II, q. 100, a. 8, no. 4.

Law and the necessary conclusions from these principles cannot suffer dispensation even by the absolute power of God, i.e., those things necessarily connected with the final end do not allow of dispensation. The reason these precepts of the Decalogue can be dispensed, according to Scotus, is because they have no necessary relation to the final end, but only a relation of convenience, a relation depending on the will of God.

A closer scrutiny of this last statement will show us the real fallacy in the theory of Scotus. The precepts which Scotus says can be dispensed are those governing the relations of man with everything that is not God; everything that does not refer directly to God has no necessary connection with the final end of man. But it is undeniably true (and we shall show this truth more exhaustively in treating of the obligation of the Natural Moral Law) that man has definite potencies that are determined, by *their very nature*, to their *own*, not to *any*, act; if they are not so determined they have no reason for existence, for a potency exists *for* its act. Similarly every act is determined, *by its very nature*, to its end; otherwise it has no reason for existence, and there is no sufficient reason for any activity whatever; moreover, this end of the act must eventually be the final end—if it is not the final end and is not a means leading to that final end it is unintelligible as constituting the term of an action. All this follows from the very *nature* of the potency and the act; and it is fundamentally true that all action and consequently all potency flow from the composite *nature* of the agent acting—otherwise the idea of specific differences of natures is meaningless. Consequently when Scotus says that everything not directly referring to God has no necessary connection with the final end of man, he is denying the determined nature of potency and act, the doctrine of specific differences, and ultimately the principle of finality and of sufficient reason.

## II. Obligation of the Natural Moral Law[76]

In his tract on the Natural Moral Law, St. Thomas does not treat of the obligation of the law. Perhaps the reason was that in the Thomistic notion, law is primarily a rule of order; the idea of obligation, while essential, is derivative, secondary. But this does not mean that the idea of obligation was overlooked, as is evident from the very derivation of the word "law" by St. Thomas from "*ligare*"—to bind[77]; it is also evident from the tracts of the *Summa* where this notion of obligation is touched upon, e.g., the treatment of the Decalogue.[78] Indeed the notion of obligation is a direct corollary from the notion of precept; granted a true precept, an obligation is *ipso facto* generated in him to whom the precept is given.[79]

Nevertheless the solution of this question of obligation involves profound and careful reasoning. Its very profundity brings out all the beauty of the Thomistic conception of law as an act of reason, especially in reference to the Natural Moral Law. An appreciation of this beauty and irrefutable logic demands a very thorough conception of this solution, a comprehension of the

76. In treating this question we have adopted the solution offered by Fr. Reginald Garrigou-Lagrange, O.P., in *God, His Existence and His Nature: A Thomistic Solution of Certain Agnostic Antinomies*, trans. Dom Bede Rose, O.S.B., 2 Vols. (St. Louis, MO: B. Herder Book Co., 1946) and Fr. Lehu in *Philosophia Moralis*.

77. *ST* I-II, q. 90, a. 1. Cf. ibid., a. 4.

78. *ST* I-II, q. 100.

79. *Quodlib.*, V, q. 10, a. 1.

very foundations on which it is based. We will accordingly start from the very sources of this solution.

Moral obligation is the result of a double necessity: namely the absolute necessity of an act in reference to an absolutely necessary final end. This necessity binds the will but does not destroy the liberty of the will, as it leaves the physical potency of acting or not acting; i.e., it binds the will inasmuch as the intellect proposes the end and the means to the will—there is no question of direct action or of coercion of the will.[80] St. Thomas speaks of this source of the moral obligation when he says: "A precept implies the notion of something due [*debiti*]. Something is due, however, in two ways. In the first way, for its own sake [*secundum se*]. And in this way it is due on account of the end, in any situation. On account of who he is [*propter se*], a doctor is obliged to foster health. In the other way, something is owed for the sake of something else [*propter aliud*]—that without which it is not possible to achieve an end. A doctor ought to prescribe a healthy diet to a sick person, without which the person could not be healed. On the other hand, something ordained to an end as rendering the achievement of the end merely better or easier—if it is still possible to achieve the end in some way without it—does not possess the nature of something truly due [*rationem debiti*]."[81]

80. Lehu, *Philosophia Moralis*, p. 220.

81. "Praeceptum importat rationem debiti; debitum autem aliquod est dupliciter. Uno modo secundum se. Et hoc modo finis est debitum in unoquoque negotio; medicus enim propter se debet quaerere sanitatem. Alio modo est aliquod debitum propter aliud; scilicet id sine quo non potest perveniri ad finem: sicut medicus debet indicere diaetam infirmo, sine qua non potest sanari. Illud vero quod ordinatur in finem ut melius aut facilius finem consequatur, si sine hoc aliqualiter possit haberi finis, non habet rationem debiti" (*Quodlib.*, V, q. 10, a. 1).

Obligation consists formally in this real transcendental relation to the last end. It is defined as follows: "the property of human actions according to which they are called necessarily postulated or necessarily forbidden with respect to the ultimate end."[82]

St. Thomas explains that the final end is as necessary in the moral order as is the first cause in the physical order and the first principles in the logical order. The participation of this final end is the desirability (*desiderari vel appeti*) of the means and the secondary ends. Without this final end volition is inexplicable. If every means were wished only as a means, every end only as a means and not for itself, the process of volition would never start and consequently there would be no activity, for it is the end which draws the agent to action.[†] Without the end there is no reason for willing the means; and as soon as an end is willed for itself alone, it is the final end, as is apparent from the very name—final, i.e., not

82. "Proprietas actuum humanorum secundum quam dicuntur necessario ponendi vel necessario vitandi per respectum ad finem ultimum" (Lehu, *Philosophia Moralis*, p. 221).

† **Editor's Note:** Steven A. Long has helpfully explained the universal implications of this point throughout his various books and articles. For example: "Without a natural end, either we could never begin to act—because there would, naturally speaking, be nothing to desire, and nothing to fear (because fear is rooted in the awareness of dangers to our possession of the good)—or, if, *per miraculem,* we could begin to act, we could never end (because our acts would lack any natural point of termination). Hence it is not simply that action without natural ends would be "bad"—that is not in the least what is at stake. Rather, it is that action without natural ends is strictly and absolutely *impossible.* We cannot even define what we mean by an efficient cause—a cause that *brings about* its effect or what is sometimes called either a productive cause, or a cause of motion—without referring to the end to which it is ordered. Try, for example to define the act of "snow shoveling" without any mention that the purpose of the act is to move snow by means of some shovel-like implement" (*Teleological Grammar of the Moral Act,* 2nd ed. Ave Maria, FL: Sapientia Press, 2015), pp. 69–70.

directed to anything else.[83] This last end is implicitly and necessarily in every natural activity; otherwise there would be no activity. Every created being tends towards the final cause as it depends from the first cause.[84] It dominates every action like the principle of identity dominates everything real both actual and possible.[85]

We have already shown that this final end, as it is in reason (*finis in intentione*) is really the rule of human actions, is the first principle from which these actions proceed. Here we are speaking of the final natural end of human nature; what does this consist in? The final end of every nature is the happiness of that particular nature; or, in more metaphysical terms, the final end is the perfection of the form of that nature, the perfect realization of the nature.[86] Since the form of human nature is the rational soul, man's final end will consist in the perfect realization of this form; moreover, since the act of the possible intellect, the act of understanding, is the highest act of this form and is precisely the act that differentiates man from the other animals,[87] his happiness or his final end consists in this act which is the highest perfection of his form. In other words, man's final end is a rational good (*bonum rationis*).[88]

This rational good appears to man's *natural* reason as desirable in itself, i.e., as "*bonum honestum*"; not something to be desired

83. *De Veritate*, q. 22, a. 2 and a. 5; *V Metaph.*, lect. 2; *ST* I-II, q. 91, a. 2, ad 2; ibid., q. 1, a. 2 and a. 4; ibid., q. 8, a. 2; ibid., q. 17, a. 9, ad 2.

84. *De Veritate*, q. 22, a. 2.

85. Garrigou-Lagrange, *God*, Vol. 1, pp. 341–2.

86. *II Sent.* d. 39, q. 2, a. 1.

87. *SCG* II, cap. 60.

88. *III Ethic.* lect. 10; *Quest. Disp. De Anima*, a. 16, *corp.* and ad 1; *ST* I, q. 62, a. 1; *ST* I-II, q. 3, a. 5; ibid., q. 4, a. 5, *corp.* and ad 3; ibid., aa. 6–8; *ST* II-II, q. 47, a. 6 and a. 7; *De Veritate*, q. 22, a. 5.

because it is useful (*bonum utile*) or as a mere source of pleasure (*bonum delectabile*). And it is so proposed to the rational appetite which *naturally* inclines to it. This appeal to reason, and consequently to the rational appetite, is solely on the grounds that this rational good is the normal perfection of man.[89] Moreover this rational good appears as the *necessary* end of human activity, its final end and consequently obligatory. And so the natural reason issues its precept, commanding man to act for this good; with the natural correlative of a command, namely obligation. This is the proximate rule of morality.[90]

This precept of reason is not free but natural; nevertheless it is eminently reasonable, flowing as it does from self-evident, yes, from first principles.[91] Asked why this obligation, the reason justifies its command by the principle of finality: "Every agent acts for an end."[92] Indeed the command "Do good, avoid evil" is nothing more than a particularized statement of "act for your end"; and this is justified on the principle of finality which we have just quoted. This principle of finality is a first principle, a self-evident truth, whose denial includes the denial of the principles of sufficient reason, of contradiction and of identity, with which it is intimately connected. In a word, this principle has ontological value.[†]

89. *De Veritate*, q. 22, a. 5.

90. *III Sent.*, d. 37, q. 1, a. 1; *II Sent.*, d. 42, q. 2, a. 5; *ST* I-II, q. 90, a. 1; ibid., q. 95, a. 2; ibid., q. 100, a. 1.

91. *De Veritate*, q. 22, a. 5, ad 3; *ST* I-II, q. 94, a. 2.

92. *ST* I, q. 44, a. 4; *ST* I-II, q. 1, a. 2.

† **Editor's Note:** Reginald Garrigou-Lagrange's study of the principle of finality remains a classic text on this topic: *Le Réalisme du Principe de Finalité* (Paris: Desclée de Brouwer, 1932).

We have said that the principle of finality is a first principle, a self-evident truth. This is easily understood if we grasp the full meaning of the terms of this principle. By "end" is here understood not merely the term of the action but the reason for placing the action (*causa cujus gratia*), i.e., a determined perfection, suitable to the agent placing the action, appearing to him as his good. Every nature has a specific activity, that is, it works for a determined end, a determined perfection suitable to the nature and indeed completing it, and this specific activity flows from the specific nature itself.[93] Since this is a determined perfection and a determined suitability to the agent—as it plainly is, indeed must be, if specific differences mean anything—it is not accidental but ordained. That is, the nature tends more to this perfection than to another. Otherwise there would be no reason why this act should be placed by this particular nature any more than any other act; there would be no reason for specifically different activity from specifically different natures.[94] St. Thomas puts this very briefly and clearly when he says:

> Every agent, of necessity, acts for an end. For if, in a number of causes ordained to one another, the first be removed, the others must, of necessity, be removed also. Now the first of all causes is the final cause.... An agent does not move except out of intention for an end. For if the agent were not determinate to some particular effect, it would not do one thing rather than another: consequently in order that

93. *ST* I, q. 44, a. 1; *ST* I-II, q. 1, a. 2; *De Veritate*, q. 22, a. 1, *corp.* and ad 3 and ad 4; ibid., a. 5.

94. *ST* I-II, q. 1, a. 2; *ST* I, q. 44, a. 4; *De Veritate*, q. 22, a. 1, *corp.* and ad 9.

> it produce a determinate effect, it must, of necessity, be determined to some certain one, which has the nature of an end.[95]

In a word, an end is the only explanation of activity; a determined end is the only explanation of a determined activity—a truth that is immediately apparent to the intellect. Indeed this principle is taken for granted in our daily lives; for instance, the very commonplace question, "Why was this done?" on seeing an action or an effect of an action, is nothing more than the application of this principle.

In the second place, we have said that a denial of this principle is a denial of the principle of sufficient reason. This can be shown very easily. The determination and determined suitability cannot be produced in the effect unless they are in some way in the cause; this is merely applying the axiom "*nemo dat quod non habet*" ("no one gives what one does not have"). This determination and determined suitability cannot be in the cause formally and actually as is self-evident; but only virtually, inasmuch as the efficient cause tends towards this effect rather than another, inasmuch as the cause was ordained to the effect, i.e., acted for that end. Otherwise we have this determination and determined suitability to the agent existing without any sufficient reason for their existence.[96]

---

95. "Omnia agentia necesse est agere propter finem. Causarum enim ad invicem ordinatarum, si prima subtrahatur, necesse est alias subtrahi. Prima autem inter omnes causas est causa finalis.... Agens autem non movet nisi ex intentione finis. Si enim agens non esset determinatum ad aliquem effectum, non magis ageret hoc quam illud, ad hoc ergo quod determinatum effectum producat, necesse est quod determinetur ad aliquid certum, quod habet rationem finis" (*ST* I-II, q. 1, a. 2).

96. *ST* I, q. 44, a. 4; *De Veritate*, q. 22, a. 1.

Not only the effect, but the action itself is essentially intentional, or ordained to an end. Without this ordination not only the effect but the act itself has no sufficient reason for its existence; the act exists for the end or it has no reason for existence.[97] We may go even further and say that the potency eliciting the act is conceivable only as essentially ordained to its act; it is for the act or it has no reason for existing. Without this ordination, we have a potency existing without a sufficient reason for its existence.[98] Our third statement, that the denial of the principle of sufficient reason is a denial of the principles of contradiction and of identity needs no explanation.[99]

Let us apply this doctrine to the problem before us. The command of the natural reason, "Do good and avoid evil," is nothing more than the command "Act for your end," since, as we have already shown, "good" here means conducive to man's end and "evil" means whatever detracts from the attainment of that end. Now the rational appetite of man—the will—is a potency whose object is the rational good,[100] i.e., the end of man. Consequently it is essentially ordained to its act, which act is in turn essentially ordained to the determined effect which is the object of the potency—the rational good of man—so that this rational appetite or will which is capable of willing the rational good or end of man, and is moreover essentially ordained to this act and object, cannot refuse to will this end of man without losing the very reason of its existence, without going contrary to the essential order of things,

97. *ST* I, q. 44, a. 4; *De Veritate*, q. 22, a. 1; *ST* I-II, q. 1, a. 3.

98. *ST* I-II, q. 1, a. 1.

99. Cf. Garrigou-Lagrange, *God*, Vol. 1, pp. 181–91.

100. *ST* I-II, q. 1, a. 3.

without losing its conformity to right reason. This is the proximate source of the obligation of the Natural Moral Law.[101]

This position is briefly and clearly proved by Fr. Lehu: "The foundation of relation is the cause from which relation rises. And yet the proximate cause of an obligatory act is because the object of an act essentially expresses a necessary connection with the ultimate end…in which the essential order consists. Therefore, the proximate foundation of moral obligation is the essential order of things."[102]

This essential order of things, or more particularly the rational good of man, is the proximate source of the obligation of the Natural Moral Law. It is a secondary but true cause in the moral order[103]; consequently, it produces a true effect, a true obligation. It does not presuppose a knowledge of God for its efficacy, since it is a self-evident truth, a first principle having an ontological value, just as are the principles of sufficient reason, of contradiction and of identity which certainly do not suppose a knowledge of God for their efficacy. Rather this principle can lead us to a knowledge of God since it contains this notion analytically and implicitly; and such a demonstration is contained in St. Thomas's "*quarta via*" ("Fourth Way") in proving the existence of God.[104]

101. Cf. Lehu, *Philosophia Moralis*, p. 250; Garrigou-Lagrange, *God*, Vol. 1, pp. 199–205 and pp. 337–45.

102. "Fundamentum relationis est causa ex qua exsurgit relatio. Atqui causa proxima obligationis actus est quia objectum actus essentialiter dicit connexionem necessariam cum fine ultimo…in quo consistit ordo essentialis. Ergo fundamentum proximum obligationis moralis est ordo essentialis rerum" (Lehu, *Philosophia Moralis*, p. 250).

103. *ST* I-II, q. 19, a. 4; ibid., ad 1 and ad 2; ibid., q. 71, a. 6, *corp.* and ad 4; ibid., q. 87, a. 1; q. 95, a. 2.

104. Cf. Garrigou-Lagrange, *God*, Vol. 1, pp. 337–45.

But if it is a cause of this obligation, it is not the whole cause. It is a secondary cause and consequently acts subordinately to and dependently from the first cause—the Eternal Law—from which it derives its whole causality. Just as in the physical order secondary causes depend on the first cause and derive their causality from this first cause, yet are real causes and produce real effects; so in the moral order the essential order of things is a true secondary cause acting under and dependent on the first cause.[105] If the first cause should cease to exist, this secondary cause would lose all causality, i.e., it could produce no obligation; and it is only in reducing this undoubted causality of the secondary cause to the first cause that it is entirely explicable and intelligible. Thus the proximate source of this obligation is the essential order of things as understood by the natural reason and proposed to the natural will; the supreme and first cause of this obligation is the Eternal Law.

It must be noted that it is quite a different question to ask what is the full reason for this obligation, what is its complete explanation and to ask does a man know he is obliged. The mere knowledge that one is obliged does not of itself include a knowledge of the existence of God, except analytically and implicitly. It is sufficient, to manifest the obligation, to show its existence by its effects, e.g., remorse of conscience, and to establish its immediate foundation; namely, the essential order of things, more explicitly the rational good of man. From there we are led to search for the supreme source of this obligation, its full explanation—the Eternal Law.[106]

105. *ST* I-II, q. 19, a. 4; ibid., q. 71, a. 6, *corp.* and ad 4; ibid., q. 87, a. 1; ibid., q. 74, a. 7; *ST* I, q. 105, a. 5; Cajetan in I-II, q. 71, a. 6 and a. 9.

106. Cf. Garrigou-Lagrange, *God,* Vol. 1, pp. 204–5. and pp. 331–45.

The Thomistic doctrine excludes the necessity of an explicit knowledge of God for the constitution of moral obligation; considered precisely in itself, in its essence as obligation of the Natural Moral Law. It does not deny that every man has a knowledge of God, at least in a confused way; in fact St. Thomas insists on this again and again and it is hard to understand how it could be otherwise.[107] It is also evident from the explanation we have just given that the Thomistic doctrine insists that this very notion of obligation, considered in its proximate source, contains the notion of the existence of God analytically and implicitly, since from this principle of finality, on which the obligation is based, we can demonstrate the existence of God. The question as to the necessity of the explicit knowledge of God for the constitution of morality is rather one of theory than of fact; but one which must nevertheless be answered clearly and logically if we are to have a correct notion of the Natural Moral Law.

From this explanation of the obligation of the Natural Moral Law, it is evident that the obligation of this law, like the law itself, is really natural. It is in no sense extrinsic, imposed on man from without, since its proximate source is the natural reason of man himself. Yet it is not the empty autonomy of Aristotle and Kant, for it is the obligation of a divine law, not a law of man; its supreme source and sole sufficient explanation is in the Eternal Law of which the Natural Moral Law is a participation and expression.

* * *

107. E.g., *ST* I, q. 2, a. 1, ad 1.

## III. Natural Moral Law, Synderesis, and Conscience

We have already shown that the essence of the Natural Moral Law consists in the natural inclinations, the light of reason and the first principles of practical reason. *Synderesis* and conscience are the steps which bring this law into concrete realization and effectiveness. *Synderesis* is the habit of the practical intellect by which it knows the first principles immediately they are proposed[108]; that is, it is a natural dispostion of the intellect to recognize these principles as soon as they are proposed.[109] Consequently it is, in one sense, innate, it does not have to be acquired[110]; but in another sense, it can be said to be acquired, inasmuch as the knowledge of the terms of these principles is acquired through the senses and of course the terms of these principles have to be recognized before the truth of the principles themselves can be seen.[111] Sylvius states this point clearly:

> It seems that they are probably right who say that it [*synderesis*] is partly from nature and partly acquired: from nature with regard to the intellectual light [*lumen intellectuale*], acquired with regard to the species received from sensible things. This is in conformity with what St. Thomas writes (*II Sent.*, d. 24, q. 2, a. 3) when he says that *synderesis* is a habit, which is in a certain way innate in our mind, from

108. *ST* I, q. 79, a. 12; *II Sent.* d. 24, q. 2, a. 3; *De Veritate*, q. 16, a. 1.

109. Thomas Pègues, O.P., *Commentaire Français Littéral de la Somme Théologique de Saint Thomas d'Aquin*, Vol. 4, *Traité de L'Homme* (Toulouse, 1909), I, q. 79, a. 12.

110. *De Veritate*, q. 16, a. 1, ad 14; *II Sent.*, d. 24, q. 2, a. 3; *III Sent.*, d. 33, q. 2, a. 4, sol. 4.

111. *ST* I-II, q. 51, a. 1; *IV Metaphy.*, Lect. 6; *De Veritate*, q. 11, a. 1.

> the light of the agent intellect, as is also the case with the habit of speculative principles (e.g., every whole is greater than its part, etc.)—although for their cognitive determination we would need the senses and memory.[112]

From this it is evident that *synderesis* is not the reasoning faculty itself but a habit of that faculty. Nor is it any essential part of the Natural Moral Law; rather the active element of the essence of the Natural Moral Law—the first principles of the practical reason—is the object of *synderesis*.[113]

Conscience, on the contrary, is not a habit but an act[114]; and an act of the practical intellect corresponding to the act of judgment of the speculative intellect.[115] It is a conclusion from the universal principles furnished by *synderesis* and a particular fact[116]; and this conclusion does not oblige of its own power[117] but by the power of its principles, i.e., the principles known through the habit of *synderesis*, and ultimately by the power of the Eternal Law.[118]

112. "Probabilius sentire videntur qui dicunt eam partim esse a natura, partim ex acquisitione: a natura quantum ad lumen intellectuale; ex acquisitione quantum ad species ex sensibilibus acceptas conformiter his B. Thomas quae (*II Sent.*, d. 24, q. 2, a. 3) scribit synderesim esse habitum, qui est quodammodo innatus menti nostrae ex ipso lumine intellectus agentis sicut et habitus principiorum speculativorum; ut omne totum est majus sua parte et hujusmodi, licet ad determinationem cognitionis eorum sensu et memoria indigeamus" (Sylvius in I, q. 79, a. 12).

113. *ST* I-II, q. 94, a. 1, ad 2.

114. *II Sent.*, d. 24, q. 2, a. 4.

115. Ibid., ad 2; *De Veritate*, q. 17, a. 1, ad 4.

116. *II Sent.*, d. 24, q. 2, a. 4, *corp.* and ad 2; ibid., d. 39, q. 3, a. 2.

117. *II Sent.*, d. 24, q. 2, a. 3, ad 3.

118. *ST* I-II, q. 74, a. 7; ibid., q. 19, a. 4.

We can now see quite easily the interrelation of *synderesis*, conscience and the active element of the Natural Moral Law—for of course there is no difficulty concerning the inclinations or the light of reason itself. St. Thomas states this relation clearly and briefly: "And in this way it is clear how *synderesis*, natural law, and conscience differ. Because the natural law names the universal principles of law; *synderesis* names their habit, or their potency with their habit; conscience names a certain kind of application of the natural law to something to be done by way of a kind of conclusion."[119]

## IV. Innate Character of This Law

The traditional doctrine that the Natural Moral Law is innate, has been a stumbling block especially for thinkers outside the Church. The true Thomistic doctrine on this matter not only upholds the traditional doctrine but removes the foundation of most of the objections urged against this traditional doctrine by a clear explanation of the meaning of this term "innate."

St. Thomas certainly held that the Natural Moral Law is innate. He says this explicitly[120]; and time and time again he uses equivalent expressions such as a "*lex impressa a Deo*" ("law

119. "Et secundum hunc modum patet, qualiter differant synderesis, lex naturalis, et conscientia: quia lex naturalis nominat ipsa universalia principia juris, synderesis vero nominat habitum eorum, seu potentiam cum habitu; conscientia vero nominat applicationem quamdam legis naturalis ad aliquid faciendum per modum conclusionis cujusdam" (*II Sent.*, d. 24, q. 2, a. 4, sol.). The *Summa* drops the idea of "*potentia*" altogether and limits *synderesis* strictly to a habit (e.g., *ST* I, q. 79, a. 12).

120. *ST* I-II, q. 94, a. 6, sed contra; ibid., q. 90, a. 4, ad 1.

impressed by God")[121] and "*lex indita*" ("an instilled law").[122] As regards the first two essential elements of this law—the natural inclinations and light of reason—there is no difficulty about their being strictly innate, and this is the doctrine of St. Thomas.[123] The real difficulty appears when we say that the third essential element—the proposition of reason—is also innate.

St. Thomas says quite plainly that these first principles or propositions are innate[124]; yet this cannot be taken strictly or it would be sheer Platonism, totally opposed by St. Thomas and Aristotle and expressly rejected by St. Thomas.[125] The key to the solution of this difficulty is given by St. Thomas in the use of another expression in describing these first principles, i.e., when he says that they are naturally known (*naturaliter nota*).[126] St. Thomas links these two ideas together in the *Commentary on the Books of Sentences*[127] when he says of these principles "*indita erant in naturali cognitione*" ("they were instilled in our natural cognition"); and he thus shows clearly just what he regards as the manner in which these propositions are innate in or impressed on man, namely, *naturally*.

It is evident from Thomistic epistemology that it is not natural for a man to have full-fledged propositions of reason from the moment of birth, as St. Thomas insists: "[the intellect] is at

121. *IV Sent.*, d. 33, q. 1, a. 2, *corp.* and ad 3; *III Sent.*, d. 37, q. 1, a. 2, sol. 1, ad 3; ibid., q. 2, a. 3; *In Job*, c. 23, lect. 1.

122. *ST* I-II, q. 106, a. 1, ad 2; *IV Sent.*, d. 33, q. 1, a. 1.

123. Cf. Chap IV.

124. *Supplem.*, q. 65, a. 1; *IV Sent.*, d. 33, q. 1, a. 1.

125. *De virtutibus in commune*, a. 8; *I Sent.*, d. 39, q. 1, a. 2, ad 4.

126. *ST* I-II, q. 17, a. 9, ad 2; *ST* II-II, q. 47, a. 6; *De Veritate*, q. 24, a. 1, ad 20; *De virtutibus in commune*, a. 8; *De Veritate*, q. 18, a. 4.

127. *III Sent.*, d. 37, q. 1, a. 1, ad 3.

first 'like a clean tablet on which nothing is written'.... This is made clear from the fact, that at first we are only in potentiality to understand, and afterwards we are made to understand actually."[128] St. Thomas shows us the real sense of this word "natural" when he says: "We must give a similar explanation of the acquisition of knowledge. For certain seeds of knowledge pre-exist in us, namely, the first concepts of understanding, which by the light of the agent intellect are immediately known through the species abstracted from sensible things. These are either complex, as axioms, or simple, as the notions of being, of the one, and so on, which the understanding grasps immediately. In these general principles, however, all the consequences are included as in certain seminal principles."[129]

Cajetan makes this idea startlingly clear when he says: "Those things which frequently occur do not happen by chance. It is clear that the universal—which is the proper motive of the intellect—is gathered *from many sensations, memories, and experiences*.... It is not, therefore, by chance—but from more frequent sense acts with regard to one type of thing more than to another—that one thing is understood before another. Again, because the senses are moved more frequently by the most universal things—even with

128. "In principio [intellectus] est sicut tabula rasa in qua nihil est scriptum.... Quod manifeste apparet ex hoc, quod in principio sumus intelligentes solum in potentia, postmodum autem efficimur intelligentes in actu" (*ST* I, q. 79, a. 2).

129. "Similiter etiam dicendum est de scientiae acquisitione; quod praeexistunt in nobis quaedam scientiarum semina, scilicet primae conceptiones intellectus, quae statim lumine intellectus agentis cognoscuntur per species a sensibilibus abstractas, sive sint complexa, sicut dignitates, sive incomplexa, sicut ratio entis, et unius, et huiusmodi, quae statim intellectus apprehendit. In istis autem principiis universalibus omnia sequentia includuntur, sicut in quibusdam rationibus seminalibus" (*De Veritate*, q. 11, a. 1).

every concurrent sensation—it is not by chance, but by the order of nature, that the intellect is first moved by the most common things."[130]

Sylvius completes the picture by showing what part extrinsic forces can play in this natural knowledge: "A good disposition of organs or sense parts—both interior and exterior—helps someone to arrive at the use of reason. But, additionally, sensible species are also required. However, their acquisition alone does not suffice. Their ordination is also necessary. And since teaching and education, or an institution, help with this ordination, even though equal in nature, children do not arrive at the use of reason at the same speed. Well-educated children generally arrive faster at the use of reason than those who spend their time among peasants or workers."[131]

The sense then of St. Thomas when he says the Natural Moral Law is innate is that, strictly speaking, two essential elements of that law are innate—the inclinations and the light of reason; as regards the third element—the proposition of reason—the word

130. "Casualitas deinde male attribuitur. Quoniam quae ex frequenti usu proveniunt, casu nequaquam fiunt: constat autem quod universale, quod est proprium motivum intellectus, *ex multis sensationibus, memoriis et experientiis* colligitur.... Non igitur casu, sed ex frequentioribus actibus sensuum circa hoc magis quam circa illud, provenit quod prius intelligatur hoc quam illud. Rursus, quia frequentius sensus moventur ab universalissimis, utpote cum omnibus sensatis concurrentibus; non casu, sed ex ordine naturae est, quod primo moveatur intellectus a communissimis" (Cajetan in I, q. 82, a. 4, no. 8).

131. "Porro quod quispiam ad rationis usum perveniat, multum facit bona dispositio organorum seu partium sensitivarum tam interiorum, quam exteriorum: sed insuper requiruntur species sensibiles; quarum tamen acquisitio sola non sufficit, sed etiam necessaria est illarum ordinatio. Et quoniam ad eam ordinationem juvat doctrina et educatio, vel institutio: hinc est quod etiam aequales in naturalibus, non in aequali tempore perveniant ad usum rationis, sed plerumque citius ad eum veniunt pueri bene educati, quam qui inter agrestes vel rustices viventes degunt" (Sylvius in I-II, q. 89, a. 6, ad 3).

is taken in a somewhat broader sense. In this last case it indicates that every man, by the very nature of his intellect, immediately and without any reasoning, knows the truth of these propositions once their terms are understood through the help of acquired sense knowledge, memory, and so on.

## V. Characteristics of the Natural Moral Law

Ordinarily four characteristics are attributed to the Natural Moral Law. It is said to be universal, that is, objectively, it is applied to all men; it is said to be evident, which is really saying that it is subjectively universal; it is called necessary because all men need guidance; and it is called immutable because it does not change. With the exception of the characteristics of necessity, we have already treated all of these topics thoroughly when explaining the nature, scope, and stability of the precepts of the Natural Moral Law. The characteristic of necessity has been treated in explaining the meaning of the phrase of St. Thomas saying that the Natural Law is a participation in the Eternal Law. Consequently, as these topics are only corollaries of the essential doctrine already given, it will not be necessary to explain them at greater length.

## VI. Criticism of Suárez on Natural Law

Suárez places the Natural Moral Law precisely in the act of reason, judgment; but he admits that the light of reason may be called the Natural Moral Law, and in another place calls it the Natural Moral Law "*in actu primo*" ("in first act"). Finally, he admits that the rational essence, inasmuch as things are naturally convenient or are not convenient to it, may be said to be the foundation of "natural honesty." Comparing this superficially with the exposition we have just given of St. Thomas's teaching on the Natural Moral Law, there would seem to be a remarkable resemblance between the two, even though they started out from general notions of law that were opposed. A closer examination of the meaning of Suárez makes it evident that this resemblance is only apparent. We might sum up the most important points of opposition in the following propositions:

NATURAL MORAL LAW

| St. Thomas | Suárez |
|---|---|
| 1. Consists essentially in the proposition of natural reason as including the light of reason and the natural inclinations. | 1. Consists essentially in the act of practical reason—judgment. |
| 2. Human nature, considered as acts are convenient or inconvenient to it, is an essential part of the Natural Moral Law. | 2. Human nature in this sense is the foundation of "natural honesty." |
| 3. The precept or proposition of natural reason is a true secondary cause producing a real effect, i.e., a real obligation. | 3. The human judgment cannot cause an obligation; it can only manifest this obligation which is the result of an act of the will of God. |
| 4. The Eternal Law—an act of divine reason—is the cause of *all* morality. | 4. This act of the will of God—Eternal Law—supposes in human acts a certain necessary honesty or malice. |
| | 5. This act of the will of God joins to this |

5. The Eternal Law and its participation in the Natural Moral Law are the cause of the whole obligation, which is divine.
6. In the hypothesis that God never issued this precept which is the Eternal Law and the Natural Moral Law, there would be no honesty or malice; for these consist formally in the accord or discord of human acts with a law or precept.
7. In the absence of this divine precept these acts have no morality.
8. Human act has goodness or malice according as it harmonizes with right reason considered as the secondary and proximate rule of morality, subordinate to and dependent on the first rule—the Eternal Law.
9. This morality of human acts according as they harmonize with right reason is the morality

necessary honesty or malice a special divine obligation.

6. In the hypothesis that God never prohibited or commanded, we could conclude that the natural honesty or malice of human acts does not consist formally in the discord or accord with any proper law or precept.
7. In the hypothesis of the absence of this act of the will of God, these acts are evil but not prohibited.
8. Human act has goodness or malice from its object precisely considered as it harmonizes with right reason; from this aspect it may be called evil, a sin and culpable without reference to a proper law.
9. Besides this culpability (from lack of harmony with reason) a human act has a special reason of good or evil "*in ordine ad Deum*" ("in order/

established by the Natural Moral Law, which is a divine law.

10. "A human act is evil through lacking conformity with its due measure: and conformity of measure in a thing depends on a rule, from which if that thing depart, it is incommensurate. Now there are two rules of the human will: one is proximate and homogeneous, viz. the human reason; the other is the first rule, viz. the eternal law, which is God's reason, so to speak.... The theologian considers sin chiefly as an offense against God; and the moral philosopher, as something contrary to reason."[132]

relation to God") added by divine law. In this way a human act is called a sin or "*culpa apud Deum*" ("guilt in the sight of God") in a special way, by reason of the transgression of God's law.

10. It is in this way that St. Thomas[133] distinguishes sin as against reason and as an offense against God; thus in this case the act would be evil, morally a sin and culpable, not however theologically "*in ordine ad Deum*" (i.e., in a case where there was no command or prohibition from the part of God).

11. The Natural Moral Law prohibits everything that is *per se* evil or inordinate

132. "Habet autem actus humanus quod sit malus, ex eo quod caret debita commensuratione. Omnis autem commensuratio cuiuscumque rei attenditur per comparationem ad aliquam regulam, a qua si divertat, incommensurata erit. Regula autem voluntatis humanae est duplex, una propinqua et homogenea, scilicet ipsa humana ratio; alia vero est prima regula, scilicet lex aeterna, quae est quasi ratio Dei.... a theologis consideratur peccatum praecipue secundum quod est offensa contra Deum, a philosopho autem morali, secundum quod contrariatur rationi" (*ST* I-II, q. 71, a. 6, *corp.* and ad 5).

133. *ST* I-II, q. 71, a. 6, ad 5.

| | |
|---|---|
| 11. Natural Moral Law prohibits everything that is *per se* evil or inordinate in human acts; without this prohibition these acts would have no morality. | in human acts; without this prohibition these acts would not have ("*ut sic dicam*" ["so to speak"]) consummate and perfect "*ratio culpae et offensae divinae*" (character...of guilt and of an offence against God"). |
| 12. The Natural Moral Law presupposes no goodness or malice; goodness or malice is the result of the obedience or disobedience of this law. | 12. This is the only law (i.e., the Natural Moral Law) which presupposes goodness and malice; other laws make this moral goodness and malice by their statutes. |

We might consider each of these propositions separately and criticize them, for example the idea of a "natural honesty" preceeding all law is an evident contradiction in terms, since a morality would thus be constituted without any norm or rule of morality and morality precisely consists in the commensuration with a rule of morality. But the falsity of these propositions of Suárez is too evident to need indication.

It would be much more profitable to seek the foundation of these differences between Suárez and St. Thomas, and consequently the foundation of the errors of Suárez. After all these are not merely gratuitous statements on the part of Suárez; they are the logical conclusions from the principles he has laid down not only on the Natural Moral Law, but ultimately from his theory of the Eternal Law and of law in general, as are also the propositions of St. Thomas the logical conclusions from his principles concerning law, the Eternal Law, and the Natural Moral Law.

Suárez, as we have seen, placed the Natural Moral Law as it is in the legislator in an act of the will of God to oblige men; as it is in the subjects of that law, he placed it in the act of human judgment. St. Thomas, on the contrary, placed the Natural Moral Law, as it is in the legislator, in the precept of the divine reason; as it is in the subject of the law, he placed it in the precept of the natural reason of man, understanding the natural reason as we have explained it, i.e., including the natural inclinations and light of reason.

Applying the theory of Suárez to moral acts, the difficulty of the essences of these acts appears at once. Moral acts are realities and consequently have, like physical realities, necessary essences—i.e., essences which cannot be changed. Since these essences depend, not on the will, but on the intellect of God and, according to Suárez, the law is an act of the will of God, it is evident that the law as interpreted by Suárez cannot be the cause of the moral essences of human acts. That this moral essence is independent of all law and is supposed by the Natural Moral Law is the logical conclusion reached by Suárez himself.

According to St. Thomas the essences depend on the intellect of God in this way: (a) the metaphysical essences depend on God's simple knowledge of His essence as imitable—"*scientia simplicis intelligentiae*" ("knowledge of simple intelligence")—dealing only with things as possible[134]; (b) the physical essences, i.e., of things actually existing at some time, depend directly on

134. *ST* I, q. 15, a. 2 and a. 3.

the Eternal Law[135]; (c) the moral essences of human acts likewise depend directly on the Eternal Law.[136] Thus St. Thomas, placing the Eternal Law, and consequently the Natural Moral Law as it is in the legislator, in the precept of divine reason, did not (in fact, could not) encounter this difficulty; he was forced to conclude logically that all morality is caused by the Natural Moral Law and ultimately by the Eternal Law. These laws suppose nothing in the moral order; they establish that order.

Again Suárez agrees that law as it is in the subject can be nothing but a thing of reason; but he also maintained that the act of reason could not be preceptive, could have none of the causality which is proper to law, because this causality, this preceptive power, is invested in the will. Consequently the Natural Moral Law as it is in its subjects, must be something of reason; but since reason cannot command, the act of reason must be merely a manifestation of an act of the will commanding and this will is the divine will to oblige men. So that this Natural Moral Law, precisely as possessing preceptive power, is something extrinsic to man.

St. Thomas, maintaining that precept is essentially an act of reason and not of will, concluded that the Natural Moral Law, as it is in its subjects, is a true (though a secondary) cause, producing a real effect; consequently the Natural Moral Law, considered precisely as preceptive, in its precise character as law, is intimately intrinsic to man. The precept of reason is for St. Thomas a cause, not a mere manifestation of the will of God as it is for Suárez. St. Thomas places two causes, each complete in its own order, each

135. *ST* I, q. 15, a. 3.

136. *ST* I-II, q. 71, a. 6.

in its own order causing the whole obligation; Suárez places two partial causes (human nature and Natural Moral Law), neither of which is the cause of the whole morality or obligation.

Since these points of opposition we have noted above are logical consequences of the opinion of Suárez and St. Thomas on the subject of the Natural Moral Law, they constitute in themselves an adequate judgment of these different opinions, indeed an eloquent judgment. We may point out in conclusion that the striking opposition of these consequences, and consequently of these two opinions, springs from the original question as to whether precept or "*imperium*" is an act of reason or of will. This fundamental question, with all its consequences, some few of which we have seen, represents the difference between the rationalism of St. Thomas and the voluntarism—a decidedly popular theory in modern statecraft—of Suárez and his school.

* * *

# Bibliography

## I. For the 1930 Edition


Billuart, Charles-René. *Summa Sancti Thomae Hodiernis Academiarum Moribus Accommodata.* Lugduni, 1864.

Frassen, Claude. *Scotus Academicus.* Rome: Ex Typographia Sallustiana, 1901.

Garrigou-Lagrange, Reginald, O.P. *God, His Existence and His Nature: A Thomistic Solution of Certain Agnostic Antinomies.* Translated by Dom Bede Rose, O.S.B. 2 vols. St. Louis, MO: B. Herder Book Co., 1946.

Gonet, Jean-Baptiste, O.P. *Manuale Thomistarum, seu Totius Theologiae Brevis Cursus in Gratiam et Commodum Studentium Editus.* Venice: 1745.

Gredt, Joseph, O.S.B. *Elementa Philosophiae Aristotelico-Thomisticae.* 4th ed. Freiburg im Breisgau: Herder, 1926.

Joannes a Sancto Thoma, O.P. *Cursus theologicus. In Summam Theologicam D. Thomae.* Paris: 1885.

Lehu, Leonardus, O.P. *Philosophia Moralis et Socialis.* Paris: Lecoffre, 1914.

Lottin, Dom Odon, O.S.B. "La Définition Classique de la Loi." *Revue Néo-Scolastique de Philosophie*, Vol. 27 (1925): pp. 243–73.

________. "Le droit naturel chez saint Thomas et ses prédécesseurs." *Ephemerides Theologicae Lovanienses*, Vol. 2 (1925): pp. 345–66.

Pègues, Thomas, O.P. *Commentaire Français Littéral de la Somme Théologique de Saint Thomas d'Aquin.* Toulouse: 1909.

Prümmer, Dominicus M., O.P. *Manuale theologiae moralis secundum principia S. Thomae Aquinatis.* Freiburg im Breisgau: Herder, 1928.

Roland-Gosselin, Bernard. *La Doctrine Politique de S. Thomas D'Aquin.* Paris: M. Rivière, 1928.

Salmanticenses. *Cursus Theologicus.* Paris: Victor Palmé, 1876.

Scotus, John Duns. *Opera Omnia.* Paris: 1844.

Suárez, Franciscus, S.J. *Tractatus de Legibus et Legislatore Deo.* Paris: 1838.

Willems, Christoph. *Philosophia Moralis.* Trier: 1908.

## II. For the 2019 Edition

Aertsen, Jan. "Is Truth *Not* a Transcendental for Aquinas?" In *Wisdom's Apprentice: Thomistic Essays in Honor of Lawrence Dewan, O.P.*, edited by Peter A. Kwasniewski, pp. 3–12. Washington, DC: The Catholic University of America Press, 2007.

__________. "Truth as Transcendental in Thomas Aquinas." *Topoi*, Vol. 11 (1992): pp. 159–71.

__________. "Truth in Thomas Aquinas." In *Doctor Communis: The Contemporary Debate on the Truth*, pp. 50–4. Vatican City: Pontifical Academy of St. Thomas Aquinas, 2002.

Allsopp, Michael E., and John J. O'Keefe, eds. *Veritatis Splendor: American Responses.* Kansas City, MO: Sheed and Ward, 1995.

Aquinas, Thomas. *Saint Thomas Aquinas: Selected Writings.* Edited and translated by Ralph McInerny. New York: Penguin Books, 1998.

Bobik, Joseph. *Aquinas on Matter and Form and the Elements: A Translation and Interpretation of the* De principiis naturae *and the* De mixtione elementorum *of St. Thomas Aquinas.* Notre Dame, IN: University of Notre Dame Press, 1998.

Boland, Vivian, O.P. *Ideas in God According to Saint Thomas Aquinas*. Leiden: Brill, 1996.

Bonino, Serge-Thomas, O.P. *Thomas d'Aquin: De la Vérité ou La science en Dieu*. Paris/Fribourg: Éditions Universitaires de Fribourg / Éditions du Cerf, 1996.

Branick, Vincent P. "The Unity of the Divine Ideas." *The New Scholasticism*, Vol. 42, No. 2 (1968): pp. 171–201.

Brock, Stephen L. "The Legal Character of Natural Law According to St. Thomas Aquinas." PhD diss., University of Toronto, 1988.

Brown, Oscar J. *Natural Rectitude and Divine Law in Aquinas*. Toronto: Pontifical Institute of Medieval Studies, 1981.

Cessario, Romanus, O.P. "Why Aquinas Locates the Natural Law within the *Sacra Doctrina*." In *St. Thomas Aquinas and the Natural Law Tradition: Contemporary Perspectives*, edited by John Goyette, Mark S. Latkovic, and Richard S. Myers, pp. 79–93. Washington, DC: The Catholic University of America Press, 2004.

_______________. *Introduction to Moral Theology*. Revised edition. Washington, DC: The Catholic University of America Press, 2013.

Cortest, Luis. *The Disfigured Face: Traditional Natural Law and Its Encounter with Modernity*. New York: Fordham University Press, 2008.

Cuddy, Cajetan, O.P. "Thomas Aquinas on the Bible and Morality: The Sacred Scriptures, the Natural Law, and the Hermeneutic of Continuity." In *Towards a Biblical Thomism: Thomas Aquinas and the Renewal of Biblical Theology*, edited by Jörgen Vijgen and Piotr Roszak, pp. 173–97. Pamplona: EUNSA, 2018.

Cunningham, Lawrence S., ed., *Intractable Disputes about the Natural Law: Alasdair MacIntyre and Critics*. Notre Dame, IN: University of Notre Dame Press, 2009.

Curran, Charles. *The Development of Moral Theology: Five Strands*. Washington, DC: Georgetown University Press, 2013.

Davitt, Thomas E., S.J. *The Nature of Law*. St. Louis, MO: B. Herder Book, Co., 1951.

Di Blasi, Fulvio. *God and the Natural Law: A Rereading of Thomas Aquinas*. Translated by David Thunder. South Bend, IN: St. Augustine's Press, 2006.

DiNoia, J. A. O.P., and Romanus Cessario, O.P., ed. *Veritatis Splendor and the Renewal of Moral Theology*. Princeton, NJ: Scepter Publishers, 1999.

Doolan, Gregory T. *Aquinas on the Divine Ideas as Exemplar Causes*. Washington, DC: The Catholic University of America Press, 2014.

Farrell, Walter., O.P. "The Law—The Facts and Explanation of the Natural Law." In *The Natural Law and the Legal Profession*, pp. 1–25. Chicago: The Catholic Lawyers' Guild of Chicago, 1950.

Feser, Edward. *The Last Superstition: A Refutation of the New Atheism.* South Bend, IN: St. Augustine's Press, 2008.

Garrigou-Lagrange, Reginald, O.P. *Le Réalisme du Principe de Finalité.* Paris: Desclée de Brouwer, 1932.

George, Robert P., ed. *Natural Law Theory: Contemporary Essays.* Oxford: Oxford University Press, 1994.

González, Ana Marta. *Contemporary Perspectives on Natural Law: Natural Law as a Limiting Concept.* Burlington, VT: Ashgate Publishing Co., 2008.

Greenstock, David L., T.O.P. "Exemplar Causality and the Supernatural Order." *The Thomist*, Vol. 16, No. 1 (1953): pp. 1–13.

Hall, Pamela M. *Narrative and the Natural Law: An Interpretation of Thomistic Ethics.* Notre Dame, IN: University of Notre Dame Press, 1994.

Hittinger, Russell. *The First Grace: Rediscovering the Natural Law in a Post-Christian World.* Wilmington, DE: ISI Books, 2003.

________. "Theology and Natural Law Theory." *Communio*, Vol. 17 (1990): pp. 402–408;

Kaczor, Christopher. *Proportionalism and the Natural Law Tradition.* Washington, DC: The Catholic University of America Press, 2002.

Keenan, James F., S.J. *A History of Catholic Moral Theology in the Twentieth Century: From Confessing Sins to Liberating Consciences*. London: Continuum, 2010.

Levering, Matthew. *Biblical Natural Law: A Theocentric and Teleological Approach*. Oxford: Oxford University Press, 2008.

Lisska, Anthony J. *Aquinas's Theory of Natural Law: An Analytic Reconstruction*. Oxford: Clarendon Press, 1996.

Long, Steven A. "Speculative Foundations of Moral Theology and the Causality of Grace." *Studies in Christian Ethics*, Vol. 23, No. 4 (2010): pp. 397–414.

________. *The Teleological Grammar of the Moral Act*. 2nd ed. Ave Maria, FL: Sapientia Press, 2015.

________. "Understanding the Common Good." *Nova et Vetera*, Vol. 16, No. 4 (2018): pp. 1135–52.

________. "Yves Simon's Approach to Natural Law." *The Thomist*, Vol. 59, No. 1 (1995): pp. 125–135.

Maritain, Jacques. *Natural Law: Reflections on Theory and Practice*. South Bend, IN: St. Augustine's Press, 2001.

McInerny, Ralph. *Ethica Thomistica: The Moral Philosophy of Thomas Aquinas*. Revised edition. Washington, DC: The Catholic University of America Press, 1997.

Pinckaers, Servais, O.P. *The Sources of Christian Ethics*. Translated by Sr. Mary Thomas Noble, O.P. Washington, DC: The Catholic University of America Press, 1995.

Porter, Jean. *Natural and Divine Law: Reclaiming the Tradition for Christian Ethics*. Grand Rapids, MI: William B. Eerdmans Publishing Co., 1999.

Rommen, Heinrich A. *The Natural Law: A Study in Legal and Social History and Philosophy* Indianapolis, IN: Liberty Fund, 1998.

Rziha, John. *Perfecting Human Actions: St. Thomas Aquinas on Human Participation in Eternal Law*. Washington, DC: The Catholic University of America Press, 2009.

Simon, Yves R. *The Tradition of Natural Law: A Philosopher's Reflection*. New York: Fordham University Press, 1999.

Sparks, Timothy, O.P., *De Divisione Causae Exemplaris apud S. Thomam*. River Forest, IL: Dominican House of Studies, 1936.

Strauss, Leo. *Natural Right and History*. Chicago: University of Chicago Press, 1950.

te Velde, Rudi A. *Participation and Substantiality in Thomas Aquinas*. Leiden: Brill, 1995.

Wallace, William Augustine, O.P. "The Cosmological Argument: A Reappraisal." *Proceedings of the American Catholic Philosophical Association*, Vol. 46 (1972): pp. 43–57.

________. "The First Way: A Rejoinder." *The Thomist*, Vol. 39, No. 2 (1975): pp. 375–82.

________. "Newtonian Antinomies Against the *Prima Via*." *The Thomist*, Vol. 19, No. 2 (1956): pp. 151–92.

________. "Physics and God: A Statement and Defense of the *Prima Via* in the Light of Modern Science." STLr. diss., Pontifical Faculty of the Immaculate Conception (Washington, DC), 1954.

Weisheipl, James A., O.P. *Nature and Motion in the Middle Ages*. Edited by William E. Carroll. Washington, DC: The Catholic University of America Press, 1985.

Westerman, Pauline C. *The Disintegration of Natural Law Theory*. Leiden: Brill, 1998.

Wippel, John F. *Thomas Aquinas on the Divine Ideas*. Toronto: Pontifical Institute of Mediaeval Studies, 1993.

CLUNY MEDIA

*Designed by Fiona Cecile Clarke, the* Cluny Media *logo depicts a monk at work in the scriptorium, with a cat sitting at his feet.*

*The monk represents our mission to emulate the invaluable contributions of the monks of Cluny in preserving the libraries of the West, our strivings to know and love the truth.*

*The cat at the monk's feet is Pangur Bán, from the eponymous Irish poem of the 9th century. The anonymous poet compares his scholarly pursuit of truth with the cat's happy hunting of mice. The depiction of Pangur Bán is an homage to the work of the monks of Irish monasteries and a sign of the joy we at Cluny take in our trade.*

"Messe ocus Pangur Bán,
cechtar nathar fria saindan:
bíth a menmasam fri seilgg,
mu memna céin im saincheirdd."

Printed in Great Britain
by Amazon

76427158R00132